RECOLLECTIONS OF MY FIFTY YEARS HUNTING AND FISHING

THE LAST OF HIS RACE

Michigan Wild Turkey Gobbler. Killed 1886. Weight 23¾ lbs. Photograph taken from the mounted bird, still a wonderful bouquet of colors.

RECOLLECTIONS *of* MY FIFTY YEARS HUNTING *and* FISHING

By

WM. B. MERSHON

1923
THE STRATFORD COMPANY, *Publishers*
Boston, Massachusetts

The STRATFORD CO., Publishers
Boston, Mass.

The Alpine Press, Boston, Mass., U. S. A.

DEDICATION

Dedicated to
The memory of my old hunting companions

Farnham Lyon, Watts Sherman Humphrey, Waldo Avery, Abner P. Bigelow, George Dan Seib, Eben N. Briggs and Charles H. Davis

Contents

Illustrations

Introductory

THERE are several reasons why I have written this book. I have hesitated to undertake it for a long time. I am aware that I can not paint in glowing colors commonplace events. I know I have very little literary talent, but I have had such a glorious time afield with rod and gun for half a century, I feel that others should enjoy some of these memories with me.

The better reason mayhap why I have undertaken to tell these stories is that in the years to come comparison can be made with the past and future, and even the contrast of today with those days I have written about is so great that the younger sportsman will marvel. Then again the history of the brook trout in Michigan should be preserved. We have much written about the grayling; nothing of the introduction of the brook trout; and how few anglers of today know that this fish was not native to the streams of the Lower Peninsula where now it is found. Little has before been written about hunting the Michigan wild turkey. I have not said much of the wild pigeon for I covered that subject about as fully as I could in *The Passenger Pigeon,* a book written by me in 1907.

A considerable time has elapsed between the writing of several of the titles of the within, and some of them have been printed in the sportsman's magazines. The reader will understand why there are some repetitions. And, too, there is a preponderance of local description and minutiæ that will not appeal to the general reader, but all of it is necessary to enable me to tell my stories in my own plain, every-day conversational way. Also it enables me to stick closely to facts, and that would not have been as easily done had I generalized more.

Some of the pictures and size of the bags will at once suggest "game hoggishness" and would be unpardonable, even if today they were possible, but in the old days they were not so regarded, and I very much doubt if the bag of the sportsman of old was any cause for the diminishing supply of wild life. Environment, and not the gun of the sportsman — I will not exempt the market hunter entirely — must be the explanation. The buffalo had to go. Had no wild pigeons been killed where could they feed in numbers now?

Wild fowl are today plentiful, yet there are few on the Saginaw marshes. The Kankakee — the greatest of all duck grounds of old — is now no longer a duck marsh. The plow has taken the place of the paddle and punt pole, as it has in countless places in the Dakotas where from ponds and marshes of fifty years ago ducks and geese darkened the sky when they arose. Our covers around Saginaw that homed thousands of ruffed grouse, and swampy woodlands and beech groves where the wild turkey dwelt are now fenced with wire and as clear and clean as a billiard table. The tangle of the rail fence corners where lurked the quail and rabbit in shelter and safety from the marauding hawk are no more, and the rail fence was the best game cover we ever had.

Another thing to be remembered before condemning the old-time sportsman for the size of his bag — do not overlook this: There was not one man hunting then where there are hundreds today. There were endless hunting and fishing grounds then inaccessible that are now easy of access. Reaching the hunting ground by horse and wagon was quite another thing than going by automobile. Today all of the game covers and fishing streams and rivulets are combed fine and close. In the old days I have written of, three-quarters of the marshes, woods, bogs and prairies never heard a gun, and the cedar swamps and far-away branches of our trout waters were inaccessible to the angler. These places maintained the supply. When the forests were lumbered, burned and cleared for the farm, when the lakes and marshes were diked and drained, when roads and Fords both came to the trout nursery in the cedar swamp, when the rail fence gave way to the barb wire, then there had to be a change in what inhabited these regions.

Future generations should have hunting and fishing. These incentives to the life out of doors should be perpetuated. It is late, very late — but not altogether too late to make the start. Game refuges, protected from fire and vermin, will do wonders. The State should own, or purchase now if it does not own, large areas and set them aside forever for the people to enjoy the grand, health-giving, mind-purifying sport with rod and gun.

NOTE: I have used in abbreviated form the names of the different railroads in the course of my narrative, although it is customary to always use the full name in a work of this kind, I presume, but we always spoke of the Flint & Pere Marquette Railway as the F. & P. M. The old Jackson, Lansing & Saginaw was the J. L. & S. afterwards owned by the Michigan Central and is today the Mackinaw division of the Michigan Central running from Jackson to Saginaw and from Saginaw to Mackinaw. The D. & B. C. was the Detroit & Bay City, now the Michigan Central. The S. T. & H. was the Saginaw, Tuscola & Huron—the old narrow gauge that ran from Saginaw to Bad Axe. That too was sold to the Flint & Pere Marquette and made a standard gauge road. Later on the Flint & Pere Marquette disappeared to become the Pere Marquette Railroad.

This explanation is made for the benefit of the readers in the years to come.

Shooting Notes

MY FIRST remembrance of going hunting other than with my father and before I could go alone, was an episode that caused quite a commotion in the household and is indelibly fixed in my memory. I think it was the only time I ever ran away from school. George Thompson, an elder brother of a chum of mine, owned a single barrel muzzle loading shotgun of unknown parentage. One day the information was conveyed to me that down by the Old Salt Works — that was the ground just below where the Carlisle tannery now is — there were lots of plover and that if I would get out of school early that afternoon, George would take me shooting, so instead of returning to my studies at the time of the afternoon recess, I skipped and George and I hiked it to the Salt Works shooting grounds.

This was the location of the first salt manufacturing institution in Saginaw and the salt was made by the solar process. Instead of evaporating the brine in kettles or pans, shallow wooden vats covered a considerable area. These vats had removable covers which rolled back and forth on wooden rollers and on sunny, fair days, the cover was rolled back and the surface of the brine in the vats exposed to the air and sun. A slow evaporation took place and formed large crystals of what is known as solar salt.

There was more or less leakage to these vats and the brine gradually ran towards the bayou, killing all vegetation, but somehow or other it made a very attractive ground for the various waders. Kildeer, yellowlegs, tip-ups and a half dozen more of the smaller sandpipers and plovers frequented this ground in the early autumn or late summer in large numbers.

The trouble was to get the birds after they were killed. George did the shooting and I was to be the retriever. The ground was soft and of the blackest, dirtiest nature. My mother was pretty particular to send me to school in clean clothes and this day I had on a suit of white cotton goods — I think she said it was marseilles — with a little golden square in it. How well I remember that suit of clothes. Instead of taking my pants off and going in bare legged, I rolled them up and of course didn't roll them up far enough, for after an unusually successful pot shot that George had made, getting quite a number of birds dead or fluttering on the bog, in I went. An unforeseen log or an extra soft spot threw me down and I was completely plastered. Neither my mother or father ever whipped any of the children. We were either sent to bed supperless or given a lecture and shamed into behaving ourselves, but I got a double dose of lecture and early bed because of both my misdeeds — playing hookey from school and nearly ruining my clothes.

Another time before I was allowed to use a gun, I

had become quite expert with the bow and arrow, and begging to go hunting, my mother and grandmother took their knitting and sat on a log while I tried to shoot the plover with bow and arrow. This was at a little marsh where the roundhouse of the Pere Marquette Railway now stands, and the old Garrison mill was nearby.

The first bird I ever killed on the wing was a wild pigeon. They frequented the Saginaw Valley in thousands from early spring until after the harvest. I had been taken with my uncle and father pigeon shooting many times to pick up birds. It was no trick for them to get seventy-five or a hundred birds before breakfast, and soon after I was given my 16-gauge double barrel gun I was taken out to shoot pigeons. The flocks were dense, as I now recall, so it was not a difficult feat to bring one down, and at the very first discharge a pigeon from my shot came fluttering to the ground. I grabbed it and admired it and was satisfied for that morning to have it my entire bag, and proudly took it home to show to my mother. It was not long before I was going pigeon shooting regularly every morning, for the flight began at daylight and was generally over by seven o'clock. Then I would get my breakfast and be off to school. My pigeon shooting continued every spring until about 1880, when it was gone forever.

Another sport that I prized very much was jacksnipe shooting. After the family had moved to the west side to be near the sawmill of which my father was the

Superintendent and Manager, I had a great deal of jacksnipe shooting. I was then fourteen years old. A water course that commenced somewhere to the north of the "Mud Road" that ran through John Winters' farm and then going southward emptied into the bayou at the foot of where Davenport Street now is, was a great game cover and was near by. After school late in September or in October I used to go down to the boggy edges of this water course and flush jacksnipe, and frequently would come home with a dozen. I had become quite expert by that time and could kill these twisters on the wing very well.

It was not long after that my father and I were running a race to see who could kill the greatest number without a miss and I beat him by killing twenty-three straight. This was on a snipe bog below Zilwaukee. I was always on the lookout for some snipe ground, and the best of all was where the marsh hay had been cut and cattle pastured. This was sure to be good ground for them. I had these places located well ahead, to be ready when the frosty nights set in and the flight was on.

The creek or marshy water course that I have spoken of that was near my home gave me occasionally a duck or two. It might be a flock of bluewinged teal that I put up in early September, or going up farther where the tree growth began, a wood duck, and among the alders there was always sure to be a woodcock, and sometimes a dozen of them.

In the early spring the high water backed up from

the river and made this a pretty wide stream. It would overflow the grassy meadows, and grass pike, or pickerel as we called them, came up to spawn and you could see them moving in pairs along the shallow margin in the grassy overflow. That was great sport for me. Taking the shot gun and old spaniel dog "Sport" who was my greatest chum, I would watch for a riffle or a protruding back fin and fire a charge of shot at it. Instantly there would be exposed on the surface one or two of these pike, belly up. Then old Sport would go in and fetch them out. He would bring five or six all right, but gradually would shake his head and spit and make all sorts of faces and refuse to pick them up. He could stand a little of the fish retrieving but not a great deal. What fun a boy and a dog can have together.

Our woodcock season began July 5th. The first Michigan game law fixed that as the opening date, and there must have been a game law when I was a boy of fifteen or sixteen, for I have no recollection of woodcock not being protected by law. Of course it was far too early, but the argument was that we must have something to shoot, that the birds were fully grown then; in August you couldn't find them anyhow and by October they were gone. In recent years we have had fairly good October cock shooting around here. My father was very fond of woodcock shooting. I never made much of a fuss about it. I remember once, however, going with Leander Lee, a local fur buyer who always had good dogs, was an excellent shot and did a great deal of shooting. It was half way surmised that he shot for the market, but if he did he was ashamed of it and never admitted it. We found them that time in the corn fields. It was hot and hard work and we met frequently and rested, but we had twenty-four birds when along early in the afternoon a farmer appeared and drove us out of the corn field, for he said he was working nearby and our shooting frightened his horses. My father once asked Leander how he cooked his woodcock and he replied that "he generally b'iled 'em." Such sacrilegious treatment of woodcock was horrible to contemplate, I judged, from the conversation that took place between my father and my mother in relation thereto.

In the early autumn golden plover frequented the fields and commons around Saginaw. I could always find them and I thought them the most delicious bird that ever came to the table. I would drive out to some field where the plover were gathered in great flocks and walk towards them. Nearly always I could get in range and get in one shot and then they would circle, giving you chance for a raking shot every now and then. A soft mellow whistle quite like the call of the yellowleg would frequently bring them within range. They seemed to have no knowledge of the source of the danger. Ten or a dozen was about as many, however, as I ever got.

Ruffed grouse shooting, next to wild turkey shooting, I considered the best of all sport. That sport has continued until this day, and I think I will leave that bird for another chapter.

At times quail shooting was exceedingly good around Saginaw. When I was a very small child, at least sixty years ago, I recall my father coming in with a tremendous lot of quail — over a hundred. He had been away two or three days down near Flint, Michigan. They were strung and hung up in the woodshed and allowed to freeze, so we had quail until long after Christmas. Then there was a long period that quail were very scarce. One was hardly heard of for ten or fifteen years, but with the more general clearing of the forests and the increase in farms, they came back again, and would be here in plenty for two or three years and then would disappear and get scarce, and so it went. Now, at the time I am writing, 1923, quail are exceedingly plentiful, but the Michigan law no longer allows them to be shot. The hard winters kill the quail, not the shooting. Snow and crust doom these birds. Only the hardiest would live through and then it was a good while before they would build up in sufficient quantity to become plentiful enough to shoot. The law protected them at odd times during these seasons of scarcity, as it should, but our legislators had more common sense in the old days, for when the quail came back, they allowed them to be shot once more. They don't do that now. The survival of the hardiest quail built up a race of strong, sturdy birds, larger than the southern quail, and they have learned to take care of themselves better. At first one found them only in the open fields — buckwheat fields, wheat stubble or a corn field in which the corn was still in the shock. That was sure to be the place to look for quail. Of late years they are rarely found in the fields, but in the densest thickets and back in the woods in the tangles of the swamp grass. My early recollection is, that upon flushing them in the fields they would scatter and hide along the ditch margin or in the grassy edges of the rail fence, but of late years this is not so. At the very first they scatter into the deepest woods so that it is the hardest kind of shooting, and not very heavy inroads can be made on any single covey. Neither have the birds become wiped out or anywhere nearly extinct in a good many years as they did in the past, because of this change of habit — taking to the woods for greater protection and because of the breeding by selection of a stronger race of birds.

I have shot quail in Texas, Mississippi, Virginia, North Carolina, Georgia and Florida, but in none of these places did I ever have as good quail shooting and as grand sport as I had around Saginaw years ago. I have come to my office and opened the morning mail and about ten or eleven o'clock taken the old dog and gun and walked out just back of the mill through the farmers' fields, not going, at the greatest distance, more than a mile or mile and a half, coming back at three or four o'clock with twelve, fifteen or twenty quail. I have done this time and again. There was no bag limit in those days. Maybe we shot too much, but

I recall one day when three of us shooting north of Merrill, Michigan, had 104 quail and a few ruffed grouse as the result of our day's shooting. The biggest shooting I ever did on quail, and while I ought to be ashamed of it I am not particularly — for birds were plentiful, and, as I said before, we had no bag limit and had not been educated to the need of conservation as we have now, was one week when I was out three times. It was near Fairgrove, a little station down on what we called the Narrow Gauge Railway, sixteen or eighteen miles from Saginaw I believe. On Tuesday I shot 32; going again on Thursday, which was Thanksgiving Day, I got 28; and on Saturday 24. On one of these days I made nearly a clean score. My recollection is that I missed only one or two birds all day. With our quail shooting we sometimes got a woodcock or two or three grouse, and the same was true when we went grouse shooting — we frequently had a dozen or so of quail to add to the bag.

There were a great many deer around Saginaw in the old times. The first deer I killed ran through our dooryard. We were then living near the sawmill on the west side. That was fifty-three years ago. I was standing at the window one day late in November; a light snow was on the ground, when a deer came running from the west, jumped over the yard fence, ran through the yard and in the direction of the river. I hastily grabbed the gun. My old spaniel dog "Sport" started with me and he took the trail and yipped ahead of me. We came to the river bank and there the deer was floundering in the ice. He had attempted to cross the river, but there was just enough ice so that he had broken through and it held him. I made a pot shot then and there, and my father, following soon after, helped me drag the deer ashore and back to the house where it was fastened to one of the rounds of an inclined lader and dressed. I thought at the time that it was a tremendous buck, but know now that it did not weigh to exceed 100 pounds. Since then I have killed dozens and dozens of deer, but none caused the excitement to me or to our household that this — my first deer — did.

It was no rare occurrence for black bear to come into the city, especially when forest fires were burning. In the fall of 1872, I think it was, we had tremendous forest fires in this part of the state. For weeks the air was so filled with smoke that it was like a fog; everyone had sore eyes. The bear, either losing their way or driven by fire, came into the city. On Water Street the old Merrill foundry stood, a long narrow building with windows opposite each other. Those to the east faced the street and to the west the river brink. A bear came lumbering down through the town, jumped through one of the windows, then out of the window directly opposite and into the river and swam across to the west side.

I am mentioning so many of these things in detail so that in the years to come whoever reads may know

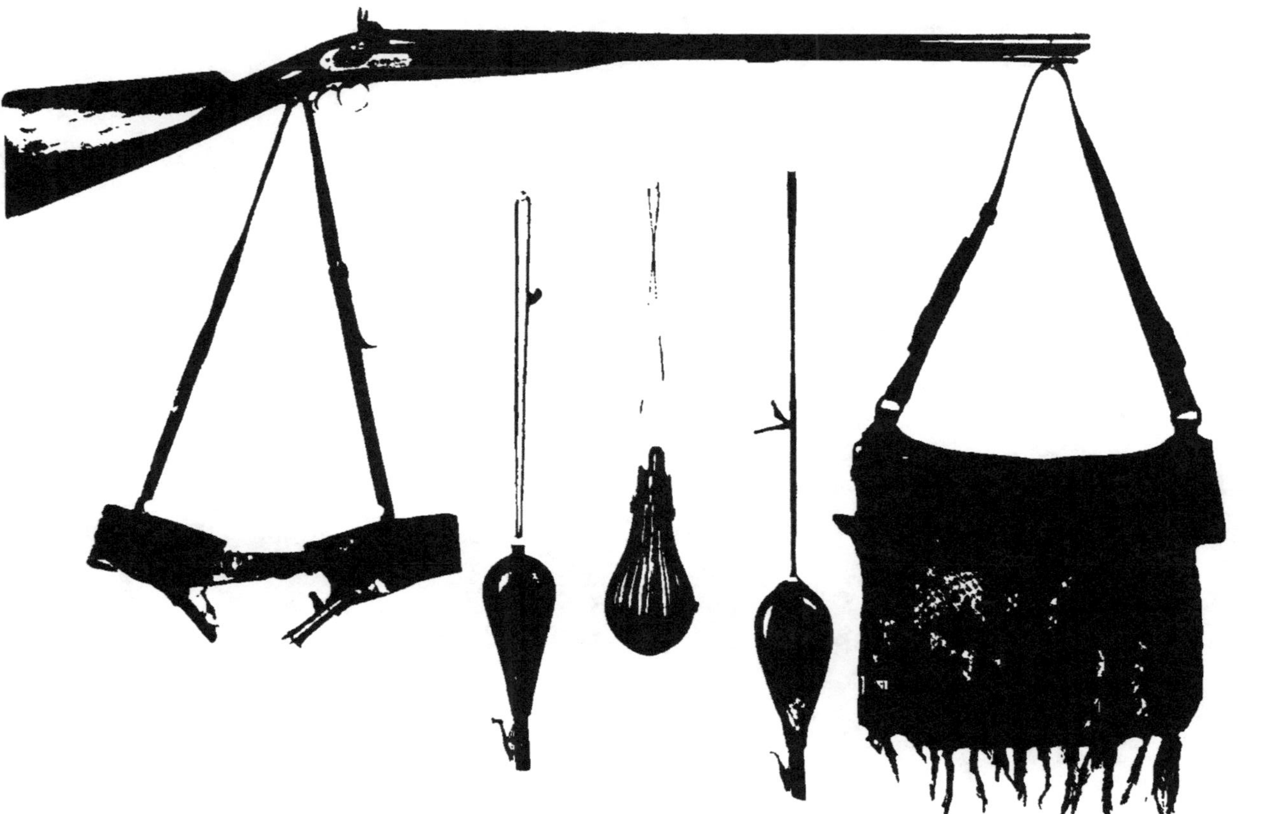

My first gun, made by Playfair of Aberdeen, 16 ga., twist barrel; ebony ramrod with brass cap. To the left, old fashioned shot and powder belt for coarse and fine shot. I never used this, but did use the leather shot pouches shown with the fluted copper powder flask hanging between. Extreme right, the old game bag.

something about the wild life near Saginaw from 1855 to about 1875, for that is the period that most of these early day happenings that I have recorded took place.

I have mentioned pigeon shooting. This was my chief sport for many years. The passenger pigeons were numerous in the Saginaw Valley from the beginning until the late 70's.

In 1907 I got together all of the data that was then to me available relative to this remarkable bird and published it in book form under the title of *The Passenger Pigeon,* and as that treated of the subject fully, I shall not say much about it here.

Every spring there was a pigeon flight. I don't know how broad the belt was. At the time I was fourteen years old I was living on the west side of the river near the crossing of the J. L. & S. and F & P M. Railways. The forest completely encircled the town and the nearest woods to my home was on the north and west, less than one-half mile away. The pigeons always came in the morning from the east side, crossed to the west side and followed the woods out to a point where would now be the intersection of the Shattuckville Road and Hermansau Street. Then they flew southwesterly to Pine Hill and thence across the Tittabawassee River, in the direction of Oakwood Cemetery. That was the original route as I recall it when I first went shooting with my uncles down near the old Saginaw Salt Works. Of course there were other flights going in the same general direction that skirted the woods on the south edge of town, several miles distant.

The birds arrived late in March and every morning this flight of pigeons going the same direction and at the same hour, namely just after daylight, the flight lasting about an hour, continued for several weeks, year after year. They must have had a nesting somewhere in the Thumb down in the Bad Axe-Sebewaing district, but we have no record of it; we don't know. That country was a long way off in those days, but it must have been a flight from a nesting to the feeding ground. Possibly the first arrivals were merely passing through to a nesting ground farther north, for we always noticed that for the first few days the flight was heaviest.

Another strange thing: they didn't return by the same route, as we found that by going three or four miles west on the Shattuckville Road we would meet a flight in the afternoon going in the opposite direction from that in the morning. My impression is that this morning flight were males, but I can not at this distance and time assert positively. Along in midsummer young pigeons appeared and we would find them on the stubble fields. The old ones by that time had gone, probably moved to another nesting, and the fact that we had these young pigeons during the summer would indicate that the first nesting was not far away.

For a bird as plentiful and in such enormous masses as the passenger pigeon, we know very, very little about its life history. The flight was not in regular flocks;

there was no leader or regular formation. They flew as it happened, one flock after another, in all shapes and at various heights. I have seen them when they were making their distance flight; that is, going to some nesting point far beyond Saginaw, pass over for hours flying in different stratas, layer upon layer, so it was possible in looking upwards to see two or three flocks in depth. These flights were high and out of gunshot. They had a habit when they came to an open commons or prairie of swooping down from above the treetops and just skimming the ground.

The passenger pigeon raised but one young at a nesting. They were gregarious and could not exist in single pairs very long. There undoubtedly were workers or feeders in the nesting that helped take care of the orphans, for it has been authentically noted that several birds came to feed one single squab. The pigeons went a long way for their feeding. The food they brought back was partially digested and the young were fed by regurgitating, or pigeon's milk, so-called. This, of course, is the only way the food could be brought back from the distance at which it was obtained. The nearby food was left for the young birds when they were able to leave the nest.

The pigeons had no regular wintering place in the south. They went wherever there was food, raising but one young at a nesting and then leaving that to shift for itself. It can readily be understood that if the large colonies were broken up and but few left to raise young how difficult or impossible it would have been for these stray or scattered young ones to have found mates, because of that habit of having no common migrating spot like many birds who migrate south to the same locality year after year.

Pigeons were considered a choice morsel in our family, pigeon potpie taking preeminence. Sometimes the young squabs were broiled, and my father used to take the breasts and corn them in brine for a day or so, take a thorn bush and stick it full of pigeon breasts and it was then inverted and hung in a hogshead and smoked lightly with hickory bark. These were put away for later use and being but lightly salted when broiled over the coals made a very choice morsel.

It was a common habit for the pigeon shooters to steal one another's birds. Shooting into a flock and only one or two birds coming down, the unscrupulous rushed to gather the dead, irrespective of whether they had done the killing or not. Frequently men went out without guns and relied upon their bulldozing to steal enough pigeons to satisfy them. I was at the mercy of these pirates when I went alone, but when I went with my father or my uncles I had a protector that could stand up for my rights. It wasn't long after I began shooting pigeons alone that I got a spaniel dog, "Sport" by name, and taught him to retrieve. After that he could accumulate not only my pigeons but some of those that the others shot, and I was always on the safe side. I used a muzzle loading 16-gauge gun, and I loaded usually with an ounce of No. 8 shot and three drams of Dupont or Curtis & Harvey's powder, using

Ely's central fire caps, the black edged felt wad over the powder and a cardboard wad over the shot. Later on pink edged wads came into vogue and I felt quite rich when I had my first box of them.

It was my custom to get up in the morning at four o'clock, go to the fringe of woods about half a mile away, and soon after the first streak of dawn the pigeons would come through the treetops. It was sporty shooting if you stood in the margin of the woods, for you had to pick out fast-flying, darting birds, singles; but if you got away from the woods a little way, then you could take a shot into the flock and trust to luck, but they flew lower within the woods, that is, some mornings. The common topic, however, amongst the pigeon shooters was as to whether they were flying high or flying low that morning, for some mornings they flew so high that very few birds were killed, but if the report spread around that the pigeons had begun flying low, then the number of shooters increased next morning. It was all over with by six-thirty or seven o'clock and I was back home for breakfast and off for school. My morning bag ranged from a dozen to twenty birds, as I recall it now. We tied them up in bunches, taking the long tail feathers, tying the tips of four feathers together, then slipping the quill through the soft part of the under mandible. After stringing six or eight birds the quills were knotted together and you could slip your finger through and carry this bunch conveniently.

The last pigeon shooting I did was at Oxford, Mich.,

a station on the Detroit & Bay City Railroad. It was two or three years after we had any pigeon shooting in Saginaw, that word came there was a flight of pigeon at Oxford, so my father and I and someone else went down there and stayed overnight and came home the next night, and I know we had two or three grain bags filled with pigeons. This must have been about 1877, maybe a year or two later.

Another sport of my boyhood was shooting squirrels, mostly black squirrels. Next in quantity were the gray squirrels and least the fox squirrels. All of the woods were filled with them, especially those woods that contained nut trees, and nearly all of our forests were well filled with oak, beech, hickory, walnut and butternut. Some of the finest oak that ever grew outdoors was cut from the forests near Saginaw — great big trees that would make a square stick of timber 30″ x 30″ x 40 feet in length. These magnificent oak trees were felled and squared with broad axes, generally by Frenchmen from Canada, and rafted to Bay City. They had to be separated by putting big pine logs between the oak to prevent the latter from sinking. Vessels came from Quebec; they had great doors or hatches in their sterns and with tackle and windlass these enormous sticks of oak were pulled endways into these stern holds. When loaded the ship sailed away to Quebec where later on, the timber found its way to the English shipyards. Worlds of white oak staves, too, were made for export to Spain. What forests Michigan had!

Once I went over to John Winter's woods, scarcely a half mile from home, and sat down. It was late in October, the nuts were falling, and pretty soon I spotted a black squirrel. I shot it, waited a moment and saw another one. I got seventeen squirrels that afternoon. All of them were out of the one big oak tree. I think the squirrels preferred the hickory nuts, just as the pigeons in the late fall preferred beech nuts.

Now and then a deer would be seen, but I did not do a great deal of deer shooting. Nearly everyone shot deer with buckshot in the old days, ran them with hounds and had no scruples about running them into the water. I think it was as late as 1878 when the records of the railroads showed that 70,000 deer were killed in the Lower Peninsula of Michigan alone. Market hunting was in vogue, the lumber camps employed professional hunters to keep their crews fed up on venison all winter long, and the slaughter was terrific. My first deer hunting trip was on the Au Gres River with Frank Millett, the engineer of a neighboring sawmill, and John Thornwaithe, who lived in Arenac, then in Bay County. We met at Whitney's mill at the mouth of the Au Gres. Millet and I went up on the old steamer *Forbes*, a little bit of a topheavy craft, and as the bay was rough I know we nearly rolled overboard. The mill was idle. there was no one around, and we made camp near by. Thornwaithe generally put out the dogs and they ran the deer into Saginaw Bay provided we did not get a shot and kill them before they got to the water. We later moved camp upstream into Au Gres swamp and it froze up while we were there and we had a dickens of a time getting out, but we had good shooting, each of us getting several deer. Another time I was invited with some older men, and one of the party objected to eating the mince pie because brandy had been put into it. He should have lived since the passage of the Volstead Act. All these localities I have mentioned are now without a tree large enough to make a saw log. What the lumberman did not get, the forest fire destroyed.

THE LAST OF HIS RACE

Michigan Wild Turkey Gobbler Killed 1886. Weight 23¾ lbs. Photograph taken from the mounted bird still a wonderful bouquet of colors

The Michigan Wild Turkey

MY FIRST recollection of the Michigan wild turkey was when my father returned from a hunting trip near Flint, bringing with him a wild turkey that was killed by a Mr. Perry and given to my father. It weighed either thirty or thirty-two pounds. That was a long while ago — somewhere around fifty-seven or fifty-eight years, but I do know that I heard my father tell my mother that it weighed either one or the other of these weights.

The last Michigan wild turkey I saw or ever heard of, was one I have been pleased to call "The Last of His Race," although it may not have been literally so. This gobbler I had mounted. He is in my possession still, as gorgeous a bird as one ever looked upon. He, too, was a gobbler, weighing twenty-three and three-quarters pounds. I will tell of the shooting of it later on.

I have other recollections of this grandest of all game birds. I had become old enough to be entrusted with a gun and had gone into the heavy tangles and thickets of the Ferguson Bayou margin. It must have been sometime late in the summer for we had summer woodcock shooting them — the season opening the 5th of July for many years. The claim was that you never could find the woodcock in August, which I guess was true, for it was their moulting time, and that by September they had mainly gone, which was not true, but they had changed location, so to get any shooting it must be had in July. The woodcock is a very early breeder and its young are full grown by the then opening day.

To return to the wild turkey. I was in this tangle after woodcock. I had a spaniel dog with me and suddenly there was a racket and out of the bushes on all sides appeared in rather clumsy flight a number of birds I did not at first recognize. I stood in open-mouthed wonder as one after the other, these awkward birds took wing and made a short flight to disappear in the thicket again. It took but a moment, however, to recognize them as half-grown turkeys. The spaniel dog had suddenly run into the brood and scattered them in this manner.

Another incident was when I was hunting partridges with my father. It was in December, for in those days seasons were long and our partridge season began the first of September and ended the 31st of December, and after the snow came we thought it was great fun going after the ruffed grouse. On this particular trip, with old Dolly drawing the old-fashioned box sleigh or cutter and warmly wrapped in a buffalo robe, we were going west along what was known as the Gratiot Plank Road.

I might digress here to say that the Gratiot Plank Road was built from Saginaw to St. Louis when the St. Louis mineral springs were in their heyday of glory, way back in the 60's, and notables from all over the country flocked to St. Louis to be cured of rheumatism and other ailments because of the marvelous magnetism of this deep well water. The story of old was, that all you had to do was to hold your penknife in the overflow for ten minutes and it would pick up a tenpenny nail by magnetism. Well, they would have a plank road for means of connection, for there was no other way of getting into St. Louis from this direction. All four-inch white pine planks were used, many of them clear pine at that. Frank Glasby had the contract. The road was under construction and was built as far as Hemlock City where we were going to spend the night at the hotel kept by Bob Sproul. How little incidents fix themselves in boyhood's mind and memory! Frank Eastman was doing the engineering work for this new plank road. It was a cold night when we gathered around the big box stove in the sitting room, bar-room and everything else of the hotel, and my memory goes back to one of his stories. I think Eastman was just back from the war where he had served with distinction in the Engineering Corps. He laid aside a pair of fur gloves as he came in and some one of the sitters around the stove attempted to put them on and I remember his stopping him. He turned to my father and said, "The only time I ever really enjoyed having a man pull on my gloves was when I was in the army and had the itch in my hands." While Hemlock City is only sixteen or eighteen miles from Saginaw, it was at that time a great center for deer hunters, many camping in the surrounding woods, and game of all kinds, including deer and bear, was plentiful.

I have digressed purposely so that the reader will recognize the tremendous change that has taken place, for now all around Hemlock are old farms and there is hardly timber enough left in that locality to hide a chipping sparrow. The old rail fence has given place to fields that are now like a billiard table surrounded with wire fences.

We left Saginaw right after breakfast and had jogged along the Gratiot Plank Road six or eight miles when ahead of us we saw turkeys crossing the road. They were only two or three hundred yards distant and there was a tremendous flock of them. My father stopped the horse and computed, from the tracks, the probable size of that flock and his conclusion was, there were about forty of them.

While the wild turkey is quite generally accorded a position of eminence, I am sure that the Michigan wild turkey was a little bit the best of any of the wild turkeys of the United States. Probably the same bird that we had here in Michigan was found in western Ontario, for I do not think they extended a great way north of the lake shore. I do not mean that the Michigan wild turkey was larger or furnished larger specimens than are found elsewhere, but as a general thing he was a sturdier, nobler bird than the turkey of the south and southwest. He must have been a hardier bird to withstand Michigan winters. To my notion he compared with the more southern birds about the same as our Michigan quail compares with that of Georgia and Florida. I think our Michigan quail will weigh at least thirty percent more than the birds I used to find around Thomasville, Georgia — big, strong-flying, hardy birds. In full plumage and the height of his glory, there was no more gorgeous bird than these Michigan gobblers. At first glance the jewels in his raiment may not shine forth, but with a little shifting so that a different angle of the sunlight strikes him, he at once is a blaze of rubies, emeralds, sapphires and opals — a perfect shimmer of scintillating color, and as to grace and shape, no thoroughbred of the turf was his equal. Wary and cunning, and most difficult to approach, yet at times it would do one of the most foolish things imaginable, almost as bad as the ostrich that hides its head in the sand and imagines it is invisible.

I never believed in shooting wild turkeys at night or as they flew out of the trees coming from their roosts, and while willing to admit that it requires skill and patience to call a turkey, it never seemed to me just right to shoot him after you had called him; as if this method lacked in sportsmanship.

We had two ways of hunting wild turkeys here in Michigan, or at least my father and I had, for it was our greatest sport. The first method was employed before snowfall, when there was no tracking snow. Take the setter or pointer that had been well broken to the game or liked it naturally — and I had one such setter in little Nippy, one of a brace — Nip and Tuck.

Tuck did not care anything about turkey hunting, but to Nippy, as I called her, for she was a little thing, it was the cream of all sport. We would go to the locality where we might expect turkeys, going to the beechnut ridges where in October we were liable to find them scratching for beechnuts, or to the edge of the woods bordering on a buckwheat field, and if Nippy got the footscent of turkeys, instantly it was made known. Her tail would begin wagging at a very lively rate and she would be all grins and smiles. She would follow along not too fast and if they had been scattered and were hiding, we would get points as staunch as though we were hunting quail, and in some instances the turkeys would lie as closely as quail, but if they had not been scattered it might be a long chase after the flock until they were scattered and then picked up as singles from points. That meant an all day's hunt, for we might go a mile or more before getting the birds scattered, and it might take hours to pick up the single birds. We would be mighty tired by the time we got back to the wagon with one turkey over a back. Father and I hunting together usually were well satisfied with one bird and that ended the hunt for that day.

The other method of hunting was tracking on the snow. The very first tracking snow — usually just before Thanksgiving Day — was the choice of the whole year in turkey shooting. My mother always depended on us to get a wild turkey for Tranksgiving dinner, for we all agreed with her that the wild turkey was so far superior to the domestic bird that they were not to be mentioned in the same breath. The pink flesh of the breast was the only apparent difference in appearance, but the flavor of our beechnut turkeys is a most pleasant memory after all these years.

So father and I would start out turkey hunting the day after the first tracking snow. It might be out the Watrousville Plank Road, or towards Frankentrost or Blumfield, up the bottom lands of the Cass River, or to the west on the Gratiot Plank Road. It didn't make much difference; there were wild turkeys all around Saginaw, but we generally went out on the Frankentrost Road in back of John Leidlein's mill and farm or over by Charlie Zilk's. We stopped on the way to have a visit with Mrs. Riedel. In the barn of some of these good old friends of ours the faithful Dolly was left. Dolly was a family horse for over twenty years. They don't have family horses any more and they miss a lot thereby. I am going to relate one trip that will illustrate the habits of the turkey.

A Day with the Turkeys Back of Charlie Zilk's

We had driven about eight miles from home and put the horse away and started down the road towards the swamp. Now the swamp in this instance, and pretty generally here in turkey country, was not a mass of cat tails, bogs and muskrat houses, but a low spot in the timber, and the forest generally consisted of black ash, elm, soft maple and occasionally an undergrowth of shrubs. The ridge adjoining might be covered with oak, maple, and beech with now and then a hickory or butternut.

Great stretches of timber land still existed back in the early 70's, the time of which I write, a half century ago, but the farmers' clearings were making rapid inroads in them. Back of the farms on both sides of the road we were traveling was a great forest and we rather hoped to find tracks of the turkeys passing from one patch of woods to the other that would decide us in the direction of our hunting.

Sure enough, when we reached the swamp with its heavy growth of grass and down timber that made such good winter shelter and hiding and feeding places, we came across the tracks of nine turkeys. The tracks had been made within an hour. That was good luck. When we were hunting turkeys on the snow we never took the dog along. Father shot a 10-gauge gun and I a 16. Sometimes we used No. 2 shot in the left barrel but more generally No. 4 and a good stiff charge of black powder.

We took the track of the turkeys and followed along, paying no particular attention to keeping quiet and making no attempt to sneak upon them, as old Bill Mathewson, who first took my father turkey hunting explained, "Go along and sing and holler and make all the noise you want to; the turkeys will sneak off to one side thinking you will pass without seeing them." "Of course," said Mathewson, "it is no use trying to sneak up on them. They will see you and you can not do it." But by following them steadily and persistently first one will separate from the flock and then another and if you take the track of one that has separated from the bunch and follow along it slowly, the first thing you know the bird will flush from almost under your nose.

We hadn't gone far before we were aware that we had disturbed the birds. They had after winding through the swamp gone up on the hardwood ridge and had been scratching for their breakfast. We could tell that we had disturbed them for they seemed to have hurried a little way and then continued more leisurely. We probably had followed a quarter of a mile when one left the flock and took off toward the swamp. We followed this track and the bird led us a merry chase as they always do. They will pick out the most difficult traveling — the almost impenetrable thickets, under this old fallen log and out through an old tree top, doubling here and there until finally you come to where the track has apparently stopped. There is a clump of smart weed all covered with snow in front of you. You can apparently see where the track has gone into one side of it, but as you stand a few yards away trying to decipher the direction it had gone from there, you see no tracks beyond this little bunch of weeds that seems barely large enough to hide a turkey, yet maybe while you are trying to figure this out there is a sudden explosion of the smart weed and almost in your very face, with the snow flung about you, rises on rapid, strong wing a great big turkey.

If you are a novice you will have buck fever. You

may shoot and you may not, and if you do shoot you can not tell afterwards in what direction you had the gun pointed when the shot was fired, but if you are an old hand at it, you will be expecting something of this kind to happen and you will keep as cool as you can and steady yourself until the bird is at the proper distance and have no difficulty in getting it down, although the old timer is occasionally fooled. I saw my father once miss a bird of this kind; he pulled off both barrels of his gun at once through some mischance. It is a wonder it did not knock him down, as he had four and one-half drams of black powder in each barrel.

In this instance, however, the bird we were following laid closely. It was my father's shot and the bird was killed — a young one weighing about ten or eleven pounds.

Father said that I should kill a turkey before we went home, so back we went and took up the tracks of the flock again. We hadn't followed far before we came to where three had separated from the others. One of the tracks was very large, evidently an old gobbler. After following for fifteen or twenty minutes they in turn separated, but I kept in the lead on the track of the big fellow. He was a cunning old chap and led me a long chase. I probably followed him an hour, through one swamp and up over one ridge and then into another swamp. Once he had flown fully three hundred yards. I got a glimpse of him in flight and knowing its habit of making a straight flight, I had no difficulty in picking up the track again. A turkey always will do this. If you don't see it in the air to mark the direction, take the direction from the last five footmarks, for he springs into the air after having run as fast as he can for five steps, giving him the momentum, I presume, to get his old aeroplane going, but you follow on in that direction and inside of five hundred yards you will pick up the track.

There was an old elm tree that had fallen with its trunk raised about four feet off the ground. The track went under this. I had just got nicely on my knees crawling under the log when out of its very tree top the bird I had been following jumped into the air. I had to hustle and scramble to get on my feet and get a shot, but I did, and had the satisfaction of seeing him tumble — a fine gobbler that after our arrival home the scales showed twenty pounds.

More time was consumed in this hunting than is apparent from the telling. I have followed an old gobbler from nine o'clock in the morning until four in the afternoon, shot at him several times during that time and yet it got away. I think that occurred with the biggest gobbler I ever saw — an old fellow that I thought surely would weigh thirty pounds. I saw him frequently but I was using a strange gun, was short of ammunition, and everything else was against me, but the greatest handicap was a case of buck fever, I guess, when I first flushed him. His enormous size completely threw me off my balance,and as it was a muzzle loading gun and I had but the two charges of coarse shot, a miss of both barrels in this case was a serious misfortune. I slipped a pen-knife in the barrell in place of shot the next time and some cuff buttons and a fishing sinker in the other barrel. I had another good chance at him a couple of hours afterwards and missed, and had to let it go at that.

For a good many years we had fair turkey shooting around Saginaw, but with the cutting off of the forests and the draining of the land for farm purposes, the birds became extinct, and I think those that lasted the longest and the final ones were the old gobblers — lone birds. We came across the tracks of one or two instead of a flock.

The Last of His Race

I think it was in the fall of 1886 that I killed the last wild turkey in Michigan. There may have been others after that date, but I have no record to show to the contrary that this bird that I got was not the last one shot.

A light snow had come the night before — not more than half an inch. Bert Beach and I had planned to go partridge shooting and we took the old Detroit & Bay City Railroad morning train out of Saginaw and got off at a station nine or ten miles out of the city (I have forgotten what it was then called) intending to hunt from there to Reese and get a train on the S. T. & H. Railroad that would bring us home about half past four in the afternoon. It was about the middle of November. We had no expectation of seeing anything other than ruffed grouse, but as it had in years past been the very heart and cream of the wild turkey district, as a precaution we each of us slipped some shells loaded with No. 2 shot in the left hand pocket of our hunting coats. We had my old Gordon setter Bob with us.

After going about half a mile from the railroad we got into a good looking piece of partridge cover and had killed one or two birds when we came across the fresh tracks of three turkeys—and they were big tracks, too. We immediately shifted our shells and put in the heavier loads and keeping Bob to heel followed the turkey tracks, but the day was turning warm and the snow melting rapidly and before we could come up with them or get them scattered so they would hide, the snow had entirely disappeared and we could no longer follow them, although we had used two hours or more in the endeavor.

Realizing that it was useless to try to find the turkeys, we resumed our grouse shooting. I know I had four or five in my pocket and Beach had about the same number. It was getting along in the afternoon and we went back into the edge of the piece of woods where we had found the turkey tracks in the morning. Beach was on the inside and I had taken the margin. Ahead of me was a big elm tree, almost at the edge of the field. It was lying on the ground with a big bushy top, and as I approached it Bob came to a point, but it was only for an instant for out of the treetop came a great turkey gobbler. He had hardly got into the air before I shot, sending a charge of No. 7 shot well into his neck and head. Only the one barrel was necessary. It was a good shot, too, for he was fully thirty yards away. Bob attempted to fetch him to me but the turkey was thrashing around like a chicken with its head cut off and although old Bob valiantly strove to haul it to me by the neck and head, it was a bit too much for him. The old fellow had fetched turkeys to me in the past. Down in Indian Territory, I remember one fell way out in the river and he swam out and towed it ashore. He was as much pleased I think with the result of my shot as I was myself. I was admiring the bird when Bert Beach came, and his congratulations were hearty and sincere. I knew I had a heavy bird and guessed his weight as around twenty pounds, but on weighing him found that I had underestimated it, as his weight was twenty-three and three-quarters pounds.

It was about three miles to Reese and we had none too much time left to get there for the home train. Tying a string to the turkey's head and to his feet made a sling that I put one arm, my shoulder and head through and started across fields and woods in an air line for Reese. With the four or five grouse in my pocket, my gun, shells and this turkey, I recall to this day what a hard lug it was, hurrying as we had to. We made the train all right and were home after a most successful day.

This bird was mounted and is in my collection of mounted birds, and although all these years have elapsed — some thirty-seven or thirty-eight — is still in perfect condition and as radiant as an oriental jewel box.

In Conclusion

Our Michigan wild turkeys rarely went into the trees, at least that was my experience in hunting them. Once in a great while if a dog suddenly rushed into a flock and scattered them, putting them on wing, one might take a tree, but I think in all my hunting experience I only once have seen a Michigan turkey in a tree.

They were very fond of buckwheat. If there was a buckwheat field in the turkey neighborhood, it would be pretty sure early in the morning that the turkeys would go to it to feed. They did not get out into the field any farther than they had to, always keeping under cover of the woods nearby, but they would scratch off the snow no matter how deep it was to get buckwheat, and the same was true of beechnuts or acorns. Then, too, they liked the swamps such as I have described before. These swampy places in the woodlands frequently had patches of coarse grasses, the seed of which the turkeys liked. No matter how heavy the snowfall, there were most always sheltered places in these swamps. A down tree along side of which this heavy swamp grass would grow made an ideal resting place and shelter for them. After feeding time in the morning (and I presume evening as well, but I never observed their evening feeding) the turkeys would go to these swamps for shelter and probably safety. I have known of their gathering in great droves in one swamp — two or three flocks assembling there.

The wild turkey never extended very far north in Michigan; in the eastern part of the state probably not beyond the Kawkawlin River in Bay County. They liked the hardwood forests, the pine and jack pine plains did not appeal to them, and the character of the land north of the Kawkawlin was a pine country pretty largely. The southern part of Michigan from the northern line that I have mentioned was well stocked with turkeys originally. The clearing off of the forests and the inroads of settlement caused their final extermination.

In the Indian Territory years ago, back in the early 80's, I had many successful turkey hunts. My companion and I once discovering turkeys feeding under the trees in a nearby grove rode rapidly amongst them; we were on horseback. The birds flew down into the river bottom where it was flanked by a high horseshoe bluff. They were scattered and we knew they would lie well to the dog. My companion had a black and tan Gordon setter, Mose by name, and old Mose gave us several points. We could have killed more turkeys but we only wanted two or three for camp use and these were easily obtained. Frequently during that fall did I shoot turkeys over points of Mose where they had been scattered in the manner as described above, but they were not our Michigan turkeys by a long shot.

These southern birds were not feathered like our

native birds were. They were lighter in color, and to my notion did not come anywhere near the average size, but they were all grand, glorious game birds and it is too bad that they are gone forever here in Michigan.

Pigeons and Squabs

Extract from Paper Read Before the Michigan Sportman's Association at Battle Creek, Michigan, Feb. 6th, 1878, by Prof. H. B. Roney of East Saginaw

"THE last but one of the prominent deficiencies of our game laws has now been reached. I refer to the yearly slaughter of fledgling pigeons, known as 'squabs,' and the netting of live pigeons for trap shooting in this and other states. In 1875 Newaygo county contained a pigeon nesting of large proportions, partially upon the lands of the F. & P. M. Railway Co. Information of the destruction of the timber coming to the knowledge of the railway authorities, an agent was despatched to the locality to arrest the work. From this gentleman I obtained my information.

"On arriving at the nesting he found a large number of persons, a portion of them Indians, some felling trees, each one of which contained *from one to fifty* nests, according to its size and branches, and others in gathering the birds. As fast as the trees fell the half feathered and fluttering fledglings, scarcely able to fly, were seized or knocked down with sticks, their necks quickly wrung, thrown into baskets, and from thence emptied into barrels. These were hauled to the station for shipment, *two and three teams* being required daily

PIGEON SHOOTING

to transport the murdered birds as fast as killed. The warehouse, a building 20 x 60 feet in size, my informant found literally full of dead young pigeons, the floor being covered in many places to a depth of three or four feet, all awaiting shipment. Over 1,500 acres of timber had been 'slashed over' in the merciless pursuit after the young birds, and the entire shipments he estimated to be between *forty and fifty tons* of 'squabs' during the nesting. The responsible head of this inhuman slaughter was a wealthy Ohio farmer who spent half his time in that business, and had for years followed up the pigeons to their nestings, from place to place, to slaughter the young birds by tons and entrap the old birds by tens of thousands for shipment out of the state, he having at that time on hand *one thousand dozen* live birds confined within some smothering lumber shanties awaiting shipment.

"At another and larger nesting in Oceana county, of which I could not obtain statistical information, residents and those qualified to speak said there were shipped *ten barrels of 'squabs' for every barrel* at the Newaygo county nesting.

"At another nesting in Grand Traverse county, in the same year, there were 900 persons employed in entrapping live birds and slaughtering and shipping 'squabs' to market. To those who have never visited or seen one of those marvelous and gigantic colonies of the feathered tribe known as pigeon nestings, these statements may seem incredible. Those who have been so fortunate will corroborate them, as my information is collected from those who have seen them with their own eyes. From the three nestings in Newaygo, Oceana and Grand Traverse counties in 1875 there were shipped to outside markets 1,000 tons, or 2,000,-000 pounds of young 'squabs,' while not less than 200,-000 dozen or 2,400,000 birds were entrapped and shipped to all parts of the United States and England.

"At this rate how long will it take to kill every wild pigeon in Michigan? Were it not for the fact that they nest two and sometimes three times a year, and consequently give opportunity for more birds to escape, we might reasonably expect their almost immediate annihilation. Sportsmen of Michigan, if we do not protect our game, who will take care of it for us?

"To the question of shooting live pigeons from a trap, I will not refer, as that does not come within the province of this article, but against supplying the rest of the United States with pigeons I do most emphatically protest. It will not be until Michigan refuses to furnish to other states her game property, that those states will turn their attention to the better construction and the better enforcement of their own game laws."

BAND TAILED PIGEON

Often mistaken for the Passenger Pigeon. This is the pigeon of the Pacific Coast mountains. Note the square tail and distinctive band.

Grouse and Quail

IT IS almost unbelievable how plentiful ruffed grouse were in this part of Michigan, and by "this part" I mean that territory in which we could get a good day's hunting either by leaving Saginaw on foot or with horse and wagon, or as we did a little later on, going out ten or twenty miles on the early morning trains of the several railroads that reached towards the four points of the compass into partridge country. On the Michigan Central south as far as St. Charles and north to Kawkawlin, Saganing or Pinconning; west on the Pere Marquette to Freeland or Smith's Crossing, or southeast to Blackmar or Birch Run; east on the S. T & H. Railroad to Creens, Kintner and Fairgrove; and last, but not least, there was the Saginaw Valley & St. Louis to probably the best and greatest of all the partridge country — around Hemlock, Merrill and Wheeler. One could go farther and still get into splendid shooting territory, but I and my companions seldom went beyond the stations named.

It was quite a long while before I learned the habits of partridge. (We generally said pa'tridge.) I hunted too much in the thick woods. Later on I found that they come out to the edges to feed. Follow along the edge of a popple thicket, especially where there was clover, or into an old chopping full of stumps, brush heaps and logs among which was growing clover, and there you were sure to find the birds, especially after three o'clock in the afternoon. Sometimes you would get them quite a distance from cover and the shooting was comparatively easy, but often the easiest shots are the ones you miss.

One time when Eben N. Briggs and myself, for Eben and I hunted together many years, were up near Freeland, we came out at a place such as I have described without realizing at that time that the birds ever came into the open. We had been shooting in the densest of thickets when old Bob, my original old Gordon setter, came to a point at a brush heap some distance from the woods. We both went to him, not expecting partridge, when first one bird and then another got up. Bob made point after point and we made miss after miss. Whether it was the novelty of it and our surprise that rattled us we never could make out, but at any rate we put up twelve or fifteen birds in about as many minutes and succeeded in killing but two of them; just as open shooting as if we were shooting prairie chickens. We made the usual complimentary remarks to each other and then followed the birds back into the thick popples. We succeeded in finding quite a number of them and my recollection is that we killed eight birds almost hand running in the thickest, hardest kind of cover to shoot in.

Briggs and I hunted the Freeland and Smith's Crossing territory for many years. We could get a train that left Saginaw at eight o'clock; it was only a half hour's run and we could begin hunting within less than a quarter of a mile of the little station and at four or four-thirty the return train to Saginaw got us home tired and happy in ample time for dinner. I think in those days, though, we called it "supper." We hadn't risen to the dignity of designating the evening meal as "dinner."

Ten or eleven ruffed grouse was our usual bag. I know that we went up five times one fall and got fifty-five birds. Another time I was there alone and came home with my pockets well filled, for I had ten partridge and quail. We always had a few quail to mix with the partridge.

I recall once I was at Smith's Crossing with Jack Morley. I had a great deal of shooting and by one o'clock when we met for lunch I had used up all of my shells. I don't know how many birds I had — my pockets were well filled — a dozen or fifteen anyhow of partridge alone and a plentiful trimming of quail. Jack had been shooting a good deal, but not as much as I, and he had not been shooting well, for he was quite blue, only having two or three birds. He was shooting a 12 and I a 16-gauge, so he could not give me any ammunition. I went along with him with my dog and when we would get a point, he would take a favorable location and I would go in from the other side and flush the bird. We were hunting back to the station, and the birds were just as plentiful as they were in the morning, and I know when we took the train we were both satisfied that we had all the birds white men should have.

I have had old Bob point quail when he was bringing another bird to me. He was a beautiful retriever, but it remained for Bob 2nd, a big, strong Gordon that I think was the best partridge dog I ever saw, to give me a staunch point on a partridge when he had one in his mouth that he was bringing to me. I was hunting with Archie McLeod near Merrill. We had but the one dog. The thicket was very dense and Bob had gone to fetch a bird that I had just killed. Archie, who was on the other side of the thicket, called to me and said Bob was on a point and he had a partridge in his mouth. I told him to go in and kill the bird. I could see the dog pointing staunchly with the partridge hanging from his mouth, but I was in no position to shoot. Archie put it up and killed it and Bob after fetching the original bird to me went back and got the second one.

Another time McLeod and I were hunting south of Merrill. We got into a lot of birds. I killed more than Archie, because he allowed me more of the shots, but we had thirty-two quail and twenty-six grouse between us for the day. These were big bags of course, but not anywhere near what the professionals or market shooters considered a good day. McLeod shot for the market in the old days, and then after the law stopped the selling of game he went to breaking dogs and guiding people and taking out hunting parties, and he was a most excellent companion. He knew the country and where to have the wagon meet us at night

— an invaluable aid to a sportsman shooting in a strange country where you had to get back to catch the evening train for home. More birds were shot in this same country for the market than any of the localities I have mentioned.

We had a lot of market shooters in and around Saginaw in those days, men who did nothing else after the season opened. There were Gary Fleming, Leander Lee, Bode and Tom Ralph. The latter killed a great many woodcock. It was said that he used to anticipate a few days so as to have a lard can or two on ice filled with woodcock by the time opening day came. A good many of them were not very technical, I guess.

I have induced C. E. Pettit, now one of the state game wardens, to give me an account of his early experiences as a market hunter. A number of the best game wardens of today were market hunters in the old days. You will recall how Jack Miner, if you ever heard him give his most interesting lecture, tells how he was a market hunter and then changed to one of the greatest game protectors that the country has ever known. Pettit's letter reads like butchery, of course, but you must remember the times. It was perfectly legal to market game, there was no bag limit, and no one realized that the cover was going to be cut off or burned off as rapidly and that with it wild life would become scarce almost to the verge of extinction. I had talked with Pettit a number of times and recalled some of his stories. I hunted one day with his brother

Rufus. He used a 10-gauge gun and a handful of No. 10 shot and shot very quickly. He gave me a race to start with. I found that I had to speed up a bit. After that I held my own with him fairly well.

So one day not long ago, I got Pettit to write a story of the old days of market hunting and here is his letter word by word. Don't criticize the individual, criticize the generation, if you will, that wasn't far-sighted enough to see what the inevitable result of unrestricted slaughter was bound to be; but read for yourself.

Clare, Michigan, Jan. 16th, 1922.

DEAR MR. MERSHON:

In looking over some of my old records and refreshing my memory, I can give you some information regarding the market hunters of the village of Hemlock during the seasons when partridge were most plentiful.

There were five of us—Edward and Hank Beamish, George Wilkins, my brother Rufus Pettit, and myself. L. Thomas & Bro., storekeepers at Hemlock, bought all the birds the five of us killed for at least two or three seasons. One season in particular I remember Thomas Bros. shipped over 4,000 birds, mostly killed by us five hunters.

The season of 1891 my brother and myself started out on the morning of September 1st, that being the first day of the open season. We made our favorite trip that we used to call "going around the world," being from Hemlock to Merrill, Merrill to Fremont,

Fremont to Hemlock, this being a trip of twenty miles by section line. That day I killed forty birds, all partridge and I carried them all in my hunting coat, this coat being made to order with double game pockets clear round. I started out with seventy-five shells and a big lunch — some load to start with. That day I should think we put up about two thousand birds. We never followed them as we could find plenty on our regular course.

The loungers at the store where we dumped our birds would make bets as to who would kill the most birds, and if any one of the five of us killed less than twenty-five, he would not show up at the store that night, but would sneak them in the next morning.

The fall of 1894, the last season for market shooting, my brother and I went to Highwood on the Michigan Central eight miles from Gladwin on the Tittabawassee. That night we made arrangements to board with the section foreman stationed there. The following morning we crossed the railroad bridge and went up the Tittabawassee one half mile to the mouth of the Molasses. We crossed the Molasses on saw-logs and found a tote road running parallel between the two rivers. We went up this road about three miles, shooting all the way up. We sat and ate our lunch and shot all the way back. On arriving at our boarding house we took inventory and found we had sixty-eight partridge. The next day we made the same trip and got only fifty-two. The third day we made the same trip, only going a little farther up the tote road. We got forty-four this day. The fourth day we tried down the river but I do not remember what we got; I know it was not very successful. The fifth day we went back up again and got around forty again, but I never saw such shooting as there was along that tote road. As soon as the dogs would point we would walk in and commence to shoot and we could see the birds flying as far down the road as you could see. The dogs would retrieve the birds on command and we would start on again with the same result. It seemed like one continuous flock. As soon as the birds took flight they would make straight for the cedar swamp on both sides of the road. We stayed at this place until we had shipped three barrels of birds to H. T. Phillips, commission merchant at Detroit.

This being the last season for market shooting, I sold my dogs and quit the business, and have killed but very few birds since.

Most sincerely,
C. E. Pettit.

Inasmuch as I am writing these recollections of the old days, and knowing in the beginning that I will be called a game hog, I might just as well be hung for an old sheep as a lamb, and am reproducing an article written by Emerson Hough as it appeared in *Forest and Stream* in December, 1897. That is but twenty-five years ago, and this hunting took place after the very best nearby partridge cover had been cleared and turned into farms, but you will recognize that it was in the Merrill district that I have before spoken of as probably the best partridge ground nearby Saginaw.

The pointer, old "Jack," that Hough mentioned was "Jack of Naso" and bred in the velvet. The Gordon "Bob" was Bob 2nd.

It was the hard winters that killed our quail. We never hunted 10% of the quail country around Merrill, and at the close of the season birds would be plentiful, what today would be called extra thick, worlds of them, but if we happened to get a bad winter, then it was all off and we would have to wait several years before we could begin quail shooting again.

Hough went with me on a number of shooting and fishing trips. Once on the Little Manistee River a bear crossed the stream right in front of him. He was with me on the Black River at Camp Higgins and took his first and only Michigan grayling. This was the last year we caught grayling. The party during that trip took about forty. The next year they were gone. I think only one was taken and that was the last grayling that I ever saw in the Lower Peninsula.

"Michigan Grouse and Quail"

"Chicago, Ill., Dec. 2, 1897.—Which he was the mayor, and they called him Pirate Bill, and he asked me to come along of him, so I came along. We took the train and rode and rode and rode till we got to the edge of the world, a place where the lumbermen had long since robbed the earth and left only stumps and burnings and slashings, all overgrown with hardwood trees and thickets and briers and brush, and with here and there a sad and solitary corn or wheat field thrusting out into the wilderness, where some farmer had gotten stranded and hadn't money enough to get back to his wife's folks. It was good, crispy, fall hunting weather. We had two good dogs—Bob, a Gordon, and Jack, an old-time meat dog, a pointer over thirteen years of age, with both front feet swelled out of shape by rheumatism and a jowl pendulous with age, but with a heart untamed by anything. We had to help Jack over the fences, and he could only waddle a few yards ahead of us, but he kept on waddling right into points on grouse and quail, and when we killed a bird he would go and bring it in like a gentleman. I had just come from some field trials, and of course the subject of retrieving is taboo at a field trial. But at sight of this venerable old meat dog with his waddle and his point and his retrieve, I felt that the world was not without its recompenses after all.

"The Pirate said he didn't care for any quail and that he was going to show me some ruffed grouse with a lot more fun. And we did find the grouse, plenty of them as that sort of thing goes — I think perhaps we put up fifteen grouse that day and bagged only five between us. But we had so much walking and so much fun with these fellows that we hardly stopped to think about the quail. Once in a while we would blunder over a bevy of quail at the edge of a slashing we were working for grouse, and would mark them down a quarter of a mile in the thicket — I never saw quail fly so far — and then we would go after them until we put up a grouse and followed off after him. Towards evening we concluded to pick up a few quail, and we found a bevy on every stubble field that we struck. We would get our double shot on the rise over the point on the stubble, old Jack and young Bob both doing handsomely for us, and then we would follow the singles into the worst sort of cover. It was hard shooting, but we found the pockets getting fuller little by little. The Pirate was a corker of a field shot, and he was fully posted on the local wrinkles of getting at the birds, so we had a lovely day. One odd little bit of shooting I remember very well. We had marked a bevy down at the edge of a little open wood, and killed one or two singles as they went up. All at once four birds sprang out together from the edge of a brush heap. Three went straight ahead and the fourth twisted over our heads and went back of us. We fired first at those going in front, and I killed with each barrel and the Pirate killed the third. Then he swung around quickly after the fourth bird, which had gone back of us, and with a pyrotechnic sort of shot killed that one also, a long way back of us, as it was topping the woods and going like a ghost. I do not think this little piece of work, on all four of the birds, would be soon seen repeated, even by so distinguished a pair of shots as ourselves. Anyhow, we did it.

"At night we counted up our birds and found that we had twenty-six in all, five ruffed grouse and twenty-one quail. We had gone over very good quail country that had not been shot very much, and we thought that we could have killed fifty birds between us if we had cared to hunt quail. Our friend, Mr. McCarthy, had poorer luck on his round, and got but few quail. Two other gentlemen were shooting at the same place, and one, Mr. Davis, with his guide, killed, if my memory serves me, nearly fifty quail that day. Mr. Davis did not care to hunt grouse. The other gentleman was Mr. Stone, who also had a local guide, and they got some twenty or thirty birds, I believe; so that all in all we had a grand lot of game.

"The next day the Pirate and I again took up our system of exterminating all the grouse, and we exterminated them just about the way we did the day before, bagging five more glorious big fellows, every one fully earned and fully enjoyed. This was the finest ruffed grouse country I was ever in during all my life, and though we did not see more than a dozen or a dozen and a half of these birds in all, we had plenty to do with these. We missed but one fair or easy shot where I let a bird get away which Bob had pointed right under our feet at a log, and which went up in broad daylight and in full view for a wonder. This bird I think had had a leg broken by an earlier shot from my companion's gun, but you have to break a leg or two on a grouse before it forgets how to fly, so we never got this fellow at all, much to our sorrow, though we put him up again in thick cover. We did not strike such good quail country this time, for the bevies had been shot into and broken up, and the birds were wild as hawks, flying to all sorts of distances when put up. Our bag that night was five grouse and only sixteen quail, I think. Mr. McCarthy improved his score this day, and our friend Mr. Briggs had better luck, getting five grouse himself and over a dozen quail. Dr. Davis and his guide had top bag, if I recollect, about sixty quail, and Mr. Stone and his man brought in over a dozen each, if the figures remain in memory correctly. I know the total was a very large one that night and showed very plainly that we were in a remarkably good game country.

"The next day the Pirate went home and I went out for a little hunt with Mr. Davis and Archie, his guide, an old market hunter. The latter I found to be a rattling good field shot. He used a Winchester pump gun, close choked, but he never lost any time getting onto his bird, and when he fired he usually got meat. I always think that a man who kills half his quail is a good shot, and that three out of five is excellent. Whether Archie can always do it or not I do not know, but I am sure he killed over 80% of his birds that day, in all sorts of cover. I don't think I ever saw any man shoot quail so well. So much could not be said for Mr. Davis and myself, who each had a bad streak. The dogs, Monk of Elmo (Tony for short) and Doc, performed perfectly. We bagged to the three guns — mostly Archie's — forty-two birds that day, I think, and of these, nine were ruffed grouse. Think of that! We killed three grouse almost before we got started. Then Archie got off from us in the wood and put up four grouse, and only killed them all! A while later we heard him shoot once in a bit of brush near by, and perhaps half an hour afterward thought to ask him what he was shooting at.

" 'Pa'tridge,' said Archie.

" 'Why didn't you kill it?' (This in would-be derision of him.)

" 'Oh, I did kill it," said he, innocently. And, in fact, we found that when he shot at a grouse he rarely did anything but kill it. It is all right to talk about the wonderful skill of this bird in evading man, and it is certainly a hard bird to kill, but after this it is in my mind forever shorn of its glory. It can not only be killed easily and in good average, but it can be killed in a great big per cent by a man who knows how to shoot. Archie did not miss any more grouse than he did quail, and he shot a close choked gun at that. I learn more about these things as I get older. Had Mr. Davis and I shot as well as Archie did, we would have had more birds than I should have liked to see. Mr. Stone and his man shot near us, but in poor luck, only getting about a dozen birds. This closed my trip, a very pleaant one indeed, with quite enough shooting in it to make it eventful.

"But this does not end the record of that country, as I shall go on to show. Since my return the Pirate has written me about a little further shooting he has had in the same spot. When I saw him last he was a very sad and penitent man. He said he had been neglecting his business shamefully, and he wished that people like me would stay away and let him make a little money to keep the wolf from the door, and not be pestering him to go shooting all the time. At any rate, not under any consideration would he go hunting again that season, for he had had enough, and knew when he had enough. Such is the disposition of man! Who has not made similar resolves? His letter does not bear quite the same tenor, for he seems to have gone out for 'just one more day,' and then two or three more, according to the evidence.

" 'We had two pretty good days, didn't we?' he says. 'I enjoyed it immensely. I feel, however, like an old bum that has deserted business entirely and become a backwoodsman. I just got back last night from seeing the season out and am glad the shooting is over with. Between now and the first of May when brook trout are ripe, I may be able to establish a reputation for hard work and attending to business; but it has been sadly shattered for sometime.

" 'My friend, Dr. S., showed up on the noon train. It rained all that day, but the next morning we took the train for our place, with Briggs and McCarthy along. Archie went with the Doctor and myself, Gladwin with Mr. McCarthy; Mr. Briggs, who likes to shoot alone, going by himself.

" 'We no sooner got over the fence than old Bob made a rush across the fields, head up. He quartered it in good style and came up like a rock; but the new dog the Doctor had brought with him had never seen a quail before, and he lit in the middle of the covey in about ten jumps, so we did not get a chance at them. Then we got into bad territory; we got up lots of birds, but they got into pieces of woods like that one you and I struck that night where we stood on some high logs, and after knocking down two or three birds we gave it up as a bad job.

" 'In the afternoon we got into better territory and got a covey scattered in short brush, and my black dog worked to perfection (I had left old Jack at home) and bird after bird was picked up; I think only one got away. Pretty soon Bob began roading, and picked up a second covey right in the same patch; they scattered close by, and we began trimming them out, when up got the third covey. We were shooting fast and furious; I never had anything like it. I have forgotten just how many the three of us trimmed out, but I think it was seventy-one birds we had in our pockets that night. At any rate, all told, the party had ninety-six, and I am quite certain that I had my share of them. (I did Archie up brown that day.)

" 'After that Archie went with Mr. Davis, and we hunted by ourselves. Mr. McCarthy was laid up with a stiff back one day, and another day there was such a wind blowing that it made it almost impossible to do anything, your fingers would get so numb, but we put in our time just the same, making four days, and we divided our birds fair and square last night and had sixty-two quail and four partridge each, that is, for each of the four. The rats or cats had gotten at one of the strings in the barn and must have used up a dozen of them. Pretty nearly slaughter, wasn't it? But the birds were there just as thick when we quit as in the beginning, and we can do it all over again another year, and hope you will be able to enjoy some of it.

" 'I have not forgotten how we knocked down those four birds that left the ground at the same time. McCarthy and I came pretty near it; three got up and we got all three of them, then struck a bunch of five partridge. We killed the first three that jumped, the other two got away while our guns were empty. We followed them up and got one of them.

" 'Dec. 2 — I dictated this letter yesterday, but there was so much to write that it did not get away. I learned of something that really makes me sad, unless McCarthy is stuffing me. He sent word last night that I missed one day of the hunting season; that the law reads: 'the first of December, inclusive;' at least, he says so; whereas I supposed we could only shoot up to the first of December. Now, isn't that too bad for a fellow that is so sadly in need of exercise and hunting as I am? It is meaner still for McCarthy to twit me about it.

" 'By the way, the last day, in the afternoon, I ran across a bit of cover that seemed to have a good many ruffed grouse in it. The first one I flushed among some burnt logs, while I was hunting out a bevy of scattered quail. I went in the woods a little further and old Bob made a fine point; the bird was killed, and he went after it. When he came in about half way he stopped, threw his head to one side, and then made as stiff and pretty a point as you ever saw, with this great, big grouse still in his mouth. This produced another bird. A little later on he made another point, which was also added to the bag. I think if I had had time to hunt that patch of wood I could have found twelve or fifteen grouse easily enough.'

"The foregoing record is a large one, though more surprising in the grand totals than for the daily scores. An average of over fifteen birds to the gun for four days is an unusual one nowadays. Many may ask how it comes that such a shooting country still exists in the north, but I may reply that this is a result of close protection. These few guns did well this year. Throw this little country open to all the guns, and half a dozen birds to the gun would be above the average. The shooting there is still good because the market hunting has stopped there, but I do not think the locality can stand even so heavy a drain as is above mentioned for very many seasons, nor do I believe that such shooting is to be predicted for any unpreserved country in the north for any very great length of time. I enjoyed most of all the sport with the grouse, of which I had never before seen so many on a hunt.

E. Hough.

1206 Boyce Building, Chicago."

Forest and Stream, December 11, 1897.

Duck Shooting

THE Saginaw River is only about twenty-two miles in length. Down its placid course has floated more white pine saw-logs than any other stream in the world. It was the main artery of river transportation for saw-logs, so to speak, for into it came other rivers, lesser arteries, that reached out through and into a large part of the pine growing area on the eastern side of the Lower Peninsula of Michigan.

From the northwest comes the Tittabawassee and into it is poured the waters of many rivers. From the southeast comes the Cass that reached the old Cass River pine territory — big, soft, glorious pine, such as the world never saw elsewhere — the cork pine of old. I have seen Cass River logs that would produce perfectly clear white pine plank four inches in thickness and four feet in width. The third or middle stream that merges into and meets the Saginaw is the Shiawassee, which also has numerous branches of considerable magnitude, such as the Flint River coming in from the southeast, the Bad from the opposite shore and farther up, and so on.

All these streams flow through what was originally a pine forest, and in the old days, for I am going back to half a century, before such a thing as a logging railroad was known, the logs were banked on the streams in the winter time and with the spring freshet the rollways were broken in and the drive began. Near the mouths of the Tittabawassee, Shiawassee and Cass were booming grounds. Great rows of spiles and boom sticks chained together made pockets and separate pens for the various brands of logs, which were stamped on the end with iron hammers bearing the insignia of the various owners. At these booms these brands were separated and sorted and done up into rafts that were held together by a rope and pin — an oak pin driven into the log amidships around which was wrapped the rope.

Then the logs were floated with the gentle current down to the booms of the owners, or the sawmills where they were to be sawn. Later on small steam tugs were employed to handle larger rafts and tow them to destination more promptly. For nearly twenty miles on either side of the Saginaw River above Saginaw City, past East Saginaw, Carrollton, Crow Island, Zilwaukee, Melbourne, to Bay City with its suburbs Portsmouth, Bangor and Banks, was almost a continuous string of sawmills, so that when the sawing season in the summer time was about over and the docks were piled full of lumber, it was almost a solid lumber pile on both sides of the river from Saginaw to Bay City, and the logs covered the surface of the water so thickly that at times it was difficult for the steamboats to find a channel, for in those days we had water connection with Cleveland and Detroit. Passenger boats ran regularly and there was an hourly service by passenger boat between Saginaw and Bay City.

How times have changed. There is not a single sawmill on the Saginaw River today cutting pine. One or two mills are sawing the remnants of the hardwood timber that half a century ago was considered worthless, and that today brings a higher price per thousand than the very best of the white pine did.

Back from the river edge, both below and above Saginaw, stretched great areas of marsh land. I don't know why I call it "marsh land," other than that it is the common expression, for this was marsh pure and simple with no land to be seen in it, tremendous beds of wild rice miles in extent, pond holes with cattails, muskrat houses, pond weed, water lilies — both yellow and white, and all the surroundings and inhabitants that an ideal old fashioned duck marsh ever contained, even to the sonorous old bullfrog that on moonlight summer nights concerted and bellowed, making a music that many a night has lulled me to sleep even in the heart of my home town, East Saginaw. Of course these tremendous stretches of marsh land meant quantities of wild fowl.

The marshes were inaccessible except by boat or canoe. Then a railroad was built from Saginaw to Bay City. Dredges went through the marsh and put up an embankment. Then more railroads followed. An interurban line rattled slappety bang through the very heart of the duck country. Dykes and ditches reclaimed hundreds and hundreds of acres to make so-called prairie farms that were hard to subdue, but when the wild grasses were finally exterminated, some of these reclaimed areas were developed into rich farms. But with all of these changes came the lessening of the wild fowl, so that where half a century or more ago the ducks congregated in hundreds of thousands, today even though there are in places large rice beds left, the ducks are few and far between and only steal in in the night-time to feed, and spend the day out on the safe broad bosom of Saginaw Bay.

Around the mouth of the Flint River was the Mishtegay. I have spelled it phonetically; I don't know what the meaning of the word is, probably derived from the Chippewa language. Then Ferguson Bayou put off from the Shiawassee and extended up towards the Flint, its earlier reaches being tremendous rice marshes. Then the shores of this bayou became fringed with trees of black walnut, elm, basswood, oak and hickory to which clung enormous wild grape vines. This was a great home of the woodduck, and black and gray squirrels innumerable. These up river marshes were miles in extent. The combined length of the two marshes I have mentioned was upwards of twenty miles, and in breadth from a mile to three or four miles. All along the margin of the river were rice fields from a few hundred feet to hundreds of yards in width. Below Saginaw the rice beds of Crow Island, Cheboyganning and Squaconning were of great area.

The duck boats then in use were canoes made from a single white pine log and were very ticklish affairs to ride in. They used to say that one had to have his hair parted in the middle to keep them balanced.

The first time I was taken duck shooting was when I was a boy seven or eight years of age. My father sent to school after me early in the afternoon, I remember, and I was told that I was to go duck shooting with my father. He was all ready and we went to the river bank where his small dugout or canoe was fastened, and his old black and tan pointer, Sport, curled up in the bow. This old pointer was a wonderful fellow — a pure black and tan and had come from Ireland, or his parents had, I have forgotten which, but he was one of the few pointers that I have ever known that liked to retrieve ducks.

My father paddled down stream a mile or so to the marshes near the mouth of what we called the Salt Works Bayou — an extensive marsh that was above Crow Island. Here he shoved the boat through a narrow lane in the wild rice to the edge of a pond hole, where he had built a blind which I recall was sort of a platform of slabs, boards and stakes well screened with rushes and rice. I don't think he had any decoys, but was in the habit of coming down here for what was known as the evening shooting. Just before sundown the ducks came in in swarms. I know he shot several and the old black and tan pointer fetched them. Then we paddled home in the evening. My father was in the habit of taking these little afternoon hunts in the fall. He was a busy man and couldn't get away from his work for long at a time, but two or three hours in the afteroon gave him such shooting as we would go long distances to get now.

The first duck that I killed was a green-winged teal, and he looked to me to be bigger than any mallard has ever looked since. I was about ten years old and was taken with my uncle to a marshy meadow where they had cut the prairie grass from a portion of it. My first gun was a double barrel 16-gauge muzzle loader, of course, made by Playfair of Aberdeen, Scotland, a beautiful weapon, and it must have been a good shooting gun, for I used it for years. The ducks were passing over this piece of marshy meadow and we were blinded, and I was instructed how to hold the gun for a passing shot, and I recall distinctly this teal passing over my head and just before he got right over me I fired and had the good fortune to kill it. I dropped the gun and ran and picked it up and gloated over it. Rarely have I made a shot that gave me more satisfaction.

My father was an excellent shot. He used a muzzle loading 10-gauge gun that I believe was made by W. & C. Scott & Sons of Birmingham. He probably had other guns before this, but my early recollection goes back to this particular weapon of which he was very fond and proud. A 12-gauge gun in those days was looked upon with little favor and a 16-gauge was only suitable for a boy. I might say in passing that I have continued to use a 16-gauge gun all my life. I never owned a larger gun. I have used that gauge for all the wonderful shooting we had around Saginaw for many years — plover, snipe, quail, grouse, ducks, etc., and in the many trips that I made to the northwest after ducks and geese it was my weapon and proved fully as effective as the larger guns that some of the members of the party used.

We used to go to Carr's Landing, a place five or six miles above Saginaw — Jimmy Carr's landing to be exact. It was a place where the land and forest came right to the river bank and one could land without having to go through an interminable distance of marsh. It was a favorite camping spot for duck hunters. Walnuts, butternuts and hickory nuts were plentiful. That meant lots of squirrels in that vicinity, so that the camp menu was varied from ducks and snipe to young squirrels fried with salt pork — a dish that even to this day the thought of makes me smack my lips.

My father had a shooting companion — Charlie Richman. They used to hunt together in one of these little canoes and take turns in paddling, one shooting from the bow while the other paddled, and early in the season this was their favorite mode of duck shooting — jumping the ducks out of the rice. One night we were camping at Carr's Landing, for as a boy I was frequently taken along even before I did much shooting. It was an exceedingly bright moonlight night and after the campfire had died down and we were trying to sleep, the quacking of the ducks made such a racket that my father proposed to his companion that they play one game of seven-up to see who should paddle for the other one to shoot and see what luck they could have by jumping the ducks against the moonlight. They went out and did some shooting, but what their success was I don't recall.

One day's shooting my father spoke of a great many times and that was when he and Charlie Richman, taking turns in this same way on the marshes below Saginaw, had killed 103 ducks in one day, which was looked upon as a big bag, as it was with muzzle loaders and but one man shooting at a time.

As to ducks. First we had the bluewinged teal and wood ducks. Then came the mallards, and last, or latest in the season, the so-called fall ducks, an expression that is used for these late comers in some sections even today. These fall ducks meant the scaup or blue bill, of which we had both the greater and the lesser, the redhead and an occasional canvasback, but the latter was a rare bird on the Saginaw River. Neither do I recall in those early days that we had many widgeon or pintail, and the black duck was hardly known. Once in two or three years my father might get one of these and then it was passed around as a curiosity. Later on black ducks began to increase. Where formerly there was probably a thousand mallards killed to one black duck, now on the Saginaw marshes and those near by on Saginaw Bay there are three black ducks shot to one mallard. These black ducks have been steadily progressing westward until they have become comparatively abundant, not only in western Michigan but across the lake in Wisconsin, Minnesota and northern and central Illinois.

For wood ducks the favorite place was Ferguson's Bayou or some of the little woodland lagoons that jutted off from the Tittabawasee or Cass, and Swan Creek, a tributary from the west putting into the Shiawassee a mile or so above Jim Carr's Landing. That was a wonderful place for woodducks. After I had become a boy of twelve or fourteen, my father and I went up Ferguson Bayou early in the season. Our season opened in those days the first of September. We were putting up woodducks, one paddling the other and we changed places upon missing a shot. I found that my portion at the paddle was far longer than my father's.

I recall once we were woodcock shooting. This must have been early in September. Our shooting ground was along the banks of the Tittabawassee near where the Michigan Central, then the J. L. & S. Railway, bridge crosses it. An old salt works stood there. I don't know who built it in the first place, but it was afterwards run by Ed Andrews who had a shingle mill in connection. Just beyond the salt works was a wood bayou or lagoon; tag alders, red willows and saggitarius fringed the shore; a dark, shadowy place, and along its margin we were looking for woodcock. As we approached the water hole wood ducks began to get up and leave it. There were dozens and dozens of them. We did not shoot at any of them, according to my father's direction. He said, "Wait awhile, they will be coming back and we will get some shooting." We were using No. 10 shot and muzzle loaders, remember. Pretty soon a pair of ducks came back and then a few more. They kept stringing in and we, standing on the margin where we could pick up the ducks we killed, shot until we had twenty-two wood ducks, killed with No. 10 shot — the end of a perfect day's woodcock shooting.

The next ducks to call our attention were blue-winged teal. I never did much of this shooting. The best of it had passed and gone before I was old enough, but I know it was my father's habit to go down to Crow Island, and there standing on the river bank, which would be the east bank of the Saginaw River, where now the old Loveland farm is, get the evening flight of teal, for in the fore part of September these birds flew from the east to the west side of the river, crossing at that point as regularly as a morning pigeon flight, and they were there literally in thousands. My father used No. 8 shot and would frequently get thirty or forty teal in an evening's shoot, and it was all dry land shooting at that, although without a dog the birds were difficult to find in the marsh grass that was nearly knee high, but the old black and tan pointer was on the job and rarely was a bird missed.

I, with a boy friend, when I was fifteen or sixteen years old, frequently after school on Friday would paddle down the river to below the New York Works or Crow Island, or to the mouth of the Salt Works Bayou, build a fire, tip the duck boat on edge as a wind break and stay there overnight just to get the early morning shooting on Saturday, for there was no school on that day and it was my only full day in the week that I could shoot, for none of us believed in Sunday shooting in those good old times. I most always had a mixed bag, for where the drainage of the solar salt fields was, the wading birds of all kinds frequented. Then there was a choice bit of snipe marsh at the New York Works, where every year I had splendid jacksnipe shooting. In the field near by the mushrooms grew. The trolling hook taken along frequently furnished a pike or bass. We lived off the land and cooked our game or fish in the open. Those were indeed wonderful days.

In duck shooting on the Saginaw River, we of course had the market hunter, and the most noted were the DuPraw's — Louis and Jacques.

Mrs. DuPraw used to take the ducks to market. They counted the mallard as a duck at full price, but it took two teal to make one duck. I think they were sold at 25 cents apiece, that is, you got one mallard or two teal for 25 cents.

When I was fifteen or sixteen years old and we were living at the Pere Marquette crossing where now the Mershon, Eddy, Parker Lumber Yard is, my father was very busy. He was working on a salary for the old Rochester Salt and Lumber Company as Superintendent and General Manager of its business, the owners being H. A. Tilden and Marvin Sackett, of New Lebanon, N. Y., and Samuel J. Tilden, I believe was a stockholder. Therefore, when the hunting season was on, my father for several years rarely had a chance to enjoy his much beloved sport, but our taste for ducks had not vanished so we used to buy them of Mrs. DuPraw, and I can recall to this day how beautifully they were dressed. She would have them done up in white cloth and to look at, even in the raw state, made one's mouth water. Her road to market passed directly before our house, so that once or twice a week we had the opportunity to take the pick of her well-filled market basket. As a boy I thought that my mother could roast a duck better than anyone living, and somehow or other even today, no duck tastes as good as those rice fed mallards or the little blue winged teal that were split open on the back and broiled on the coals at home when I was a schoolboy.

In order to have something authentic relative to the DuPraw's hunting and shooting, Hon. Riley L. Crane has kindly written the following brief history:

"The DuPraw Marsh in Kochville Township"

"It may be of interest to people who remember the hunting conditions along the Saginaw River near the Bay County line, and instructive to the younger people, to give the following facts:

"One of the first permanent duck and fur hunters was Louis DuPraw, who came from Detroit nearly a century ago. Mr. DuPraw was born in France but came to Detroit and settled there. After his wife died, he moved to Bay City and more than ninety years ago settled on the east side of what is now the Michigan Central Railroad and one mile south of the Bay County line, in Kochville Township. The Squaconning Creek was then an open stream entering Saginaw River about a mile west of the present interurban bridge and extended southerly one mile, then in a westerly course through the easterly half of Kochville Township, and is known as Davis' Creek. The hunting at this point was so attractive to Mr. DuPraw that he sold his property in Detroit, that later was worth a very large sum. The first year upon this new and before uninhabited land, he grew a good crop of corn, potatoes and other spring crops and was well pleased with his location, for ducks and fur bearing animals were at hand in abundance.

"The next summer he was completely drowned out and was forced to move back to Bay City, and the flags grew that season higher than a man's head where his crops were the summer before. Not discouraged he soon returned, moving up the river to Davis' Creek, about two miles southwest of his first location, where he cleared a farm and resided until his death in the 80's. He was a man of great endurance, pronounced character and bravery. He killed a bear with a hand axe in this marsh, the only event of the kind. Mr. DuPraw ceased to hunt after reaching middle age and devoted his time to his farm and died at the age of eighty-four years.

"His two sons, Louis and Jacques, took up hunting in an early day upon this marsh and followed it until they died a few years ago. Each had a farm adjoining the old homestead but they pressed the market hunting more than any other two men in the community. The ducks were plentiful in this marsh during the spring and fall and perhaps no better shooting ground could be found in the country. Being south of the lake and Saginaw Bay, it was a natural feeding place for ducks, and the northerly winds making the lake and bay water rough, the birds would come to this marsh in great numbers with northerly winds, especially in the fall season. The wild rice was abundant and furnished excellent feed for the wild ducks, an indispensable factor in any good shooting ground. Ducks will not harbor when disturbed, unless it is their feeding place.

"The gray mallard and blue winged teal predominated in the early days and furnished the bulk of market supply from this marsh. There were varieties of other ducks — the black duck, green winged teal, wood duck and various varieties of fall ducks, but the gray mallard, the drake having a beautiful green head and green and brown stripes, was a handsome bird and furnished splendid food. For the last twenty-five years, the black duck has, to a large measure, superseded the gray mallard in this marsh, and the blue winged teal has diminished in numbers rapidly.

"The boat used here by the early hunters was the dugout canoe — a pine tree dug out somewhat like a trough — and not too steady, but often easily upset.

"The largest number of ducks shot upon this marsh by a single charge were nineteen blue winged teal shot on the fly by Jacques DuPraw with a single barrel, muzzle-loading shot gun. The greatest number of ducks killed there in a single day by two men was two hundred and seventy-two birds, about 1876, Mr. Louis DuPraw getting one hundred and sixty-two with a 10-gauge breech-loading shot gun and Mr. Jacques Dupraw one hundred and ten with 12-gauge, double barrel, muzzle-loading gun.

"These hunters found no hardship too great to overcome in making a successful hunt. It was not an unusual thing for them to take off their pants, wade through the marsh to a duck pond, carrying their gun and clothing above the water, and then go upon a bog or muskrat house and dress themselves and remain there shooting for hours, even when the weather was cold so as to produce ice and snow. It was the claim of the DuPraws that in good hunting they could average a duck a minute during the time they were shooting. It was not an uncommon thing for the hunters to bring their boats filled with ducks, but now many a hunter is happy if he returns with a single duck, and should he get a pair or two he is very proud.

"Up to twenty-five years ago, the blue winged teal and gray mallard hatched in this marsh, but of late very little brooding is done in that vicinity. Wild geese were upon this territory, spring and fall, and even now visit, in a small way. In early days the beautiful white swan was often seen there and sometimes in considerable numbers, especially when the water was high.

"In the early days many creeks and water courses cut through this marsh, which made it easy for the hunter to pass and also furnished abundance of wild rice and splendid feeding and resting places for the birds. It was a natural and accessible hunting ground for birds, muskrat and mink, probably not excelled in productiveness for the same extent of land anywhere in the country. It was a natural resting and feeding place for birds going to and fro in their traveling season and a natural home for muskrat, mink and coon. This ground was principally a marsh with clay bottom and black mucky top soil, but in places was sufficiently high for large trees to grow, or a prairie that could be cropped. However, usually the entire body was covered with water in the spring and early summer, so no one resided upon this territory until recently. It was the resort of deer, bear and foxes in large numbers and especially in dry seasons until thirty years ago.

"One can judge of the abundance of fur bearing animals when we learn that Jacques and Louis DuPraw each trapped and speared from 1,000 to 2,000 muskrats each year while they hunted this property. Conditions have changed, and especially since the interurban railway was built across this hunting ground near its center.

"In the 70's the wild pigeon was in abundance in the hardwood near this marsh, but they have entirely disappeared. Birds and fur animals must be protected and it is evident, if not cared for, will in the future become extinct. This place was an ideal hunting ground, but alas, no more as it was in the days of old.

"RILEY L. CRANE."

The duck marshes on the Saginaw River no longer teem with water fowl. In early September and before the first frost the cackle of the Carolina rail is on every hand. These little birds — the Sora, seem as plentiful as ever, so I have not given up the marshes of the Saginaw entirely, but once or twice in the early part of September I get out the old canoe and with Alphonse to paddle or push, I take the trip through several miles of the Cheboyganning rice beds and usually get what the law allows of rail shooting, but in making all of this distance through acres and acres of rice, one or two ducks maybe is all I see in place of the thousands of old.

The Witchery of the Saginaw Marshes

TO ME the marsh has been a place of contentment and joy. Whether in the early September opening days of the duck season when the native birds only are to be expected, or the crisp Indian summer haze of October overspreads the droning silence and the first "fall ducks" are in from the north, or later when the blustering gales and snow squalls of November make one put on the warmest of clothing and crouch beside the shelter of a blind or tangle of marsh growth to keep off the biting cold winds, always there is a joy and contentment creeps over me in the great solitude and long vision expanse of the marsh. There is so much to see, so much to listen to, or for, so much to speculate about and hope for, that there is no place that my days afield or tramps afar take me in quest of other game that quite brings the contentment, peace and satisfaction that the day on the marsh can bring to him who will give himself to its full enjoyment if he is observing and loves nature, as all true sportsmen must, and has the happy trait of counting the size of the bag as least.

Years back the duck season began September 1st, and many blue winged teal and mallards, that we called gray ducks, raised their broods on our home marshes. The rice was high, still in the milk; water lilies, both white and yellow, filled the open places; the pickerel weed with its blue spikes had not yet lost its beauty. The redwinged blackbirds had flocked in clouds, and taking wing were uncountable and for brief moments darkened the skyline. Then as quickly as they had appeared from nowhere, they were out of sight again, but listen! What a concert you can hear from the dense rice cover, for when the rice is in the milk these cheery birds love it best.

Hunting ducks now is mostly by jumping them by punting or paddling the little, totterish canoe or duck boat along the edge of the rice. No frost has come to cause it to fall and it is almost impossible to punt the boat through its denseness. One in the bow to shoot, one in the stern to push or paddle, we as quietly as possible creep along. It is hard to shove into the rice for the dead birds and hard to mark the spot where they fall, and if only wing broken the quest is almost hopeless. When I was fortunate and had Frank Allore with me or one of his sons, Ed or young Frank, my troubles were few, for they were to the marsh born — French muskrat trappers and hunters all their lives.

To one side the teal are alighting. "There must be a pond hole in there; let's see if we can get in." A way is found, one lead after another. Bitterns or shitepokes, as they are called, with squawk and intestinal evacuation spring into the air, startling one so that the gun flies to the shoulder involuntarily. A great pike or carp sunning himself at the surface whirls and with its unexpected noisy splurge gives your tensioned nerves another jump. With good luck you reach a spot where the pond hole is only hidden by a few more yards of rice and you know the teal are close by and probably hundreds of them. A momentary question goes through your mind. "Shall I give them the first barrel on the water?" It is dismissed almost as soon, for early I have been taught it is not the way of the sportsman. Give the birds a chance is the rule. Yet I can not help hoping they will be well bunched and I can get more than one with the first barrel and hope for another with my second. Well, sometimes it works one way and sometimes another. Either way it's the life worth living.

We push into the rice and have our lunch. A marsh wren dodges in and out and cocks its tail much like its cousin of our back door nesting box. A least bittern is standing on a lily pad not far away looking at the sky. Coots are paddling about in the open pond hole we have just left and the teal are coming back. It surely is a favorite feeding ground, or more likely a good sleeping place this hot day, for the little, round-bodied blue wings. Mosquitoes bother so we do not tarry long but get outside where there is more air and hope for a breeze.

When the boat is thumped with the paddle or a mill whistle calls the men back from the noon hour, Soras answer in derision all around and from afar. It is early for them yet. Wait until there are frosty nights up north, about the middle of September, then these gay and airy little marsh dwellers will be daintily treading the lily pads picking up the rice that has ripened and fallen upon the great outstretched leaf carpet of the ponds, not in single thousands but in hundreds of thousands. Now a bullfrog and its companion, the cowfrog, call a deep bass booming that one can not tell whether it is far or near.

We are homeward bound before sundown, not staying to see the increased movement of the water birds at nightfall, but we know there will be singles and flocks coming in to the night feeding spots. Great blue herons on lazy wings are overhead moving to some distant marsh — a regular habit of these ungainly birds in September. Afternoon or early evening will mark the flight over the same pathway for weeks, the heron going from the marshes of the lower river to the great expanse of rice and cattail above the city, a ten or twelve mile flight, to return early the next morning.

The sky is red in the west. The end has come to a perfect day on the marsh.

October has come. We are out earlier now, for the redheads are here, pintail and widgeon too and mayhap a green winged teal and blue bill or scaup. So we must try for the morning flight over decoys. It is chilly as we are early away. We go to a blind prepared some days before that the ducks have had time to become used to. If the wind is brisk and the place well chosen we may have good sport. The coots are thicker now than in early September and are destroying acres of wild celery before the canvasbacks will be down to get it. How they skitter along the water ahead of the boat. Gallinules too are plentiful and fly from every little island of rush and reed to the shelter of the shore growths. Alighting, they seem to drop stern end first as if out of breath and could not go a rod farther. The Sora or Carolina rail have been hurried south because of a frost a few nights ago. Most of the blue winged teal also have gone, but not all, for now and then a few get up out of the ripened lily pads. A jack-snipe scaips away from a bog as we pass. The blue heron and bittern are with us still. Sandpipers and plovers of various sorts have stopped to feed and then move on to warmer climes.

By mid-forenoon the duck movement lags. The day is warm; a smoky haze hangs over the marsh and to where the forest edge shows maples with leaves reddening. Your face tickles from cobwebs that the air is carrying in wondrous threads; they hang on cattail and rush. The rice has ripened and fallen. Now it is easy to push a boat through it, so let us leave the blind and try to jump mallards and black ducks from its beds or the bog holes along the margin. The musk-rats are just starting to build their houses. They yet have plenty of time before they will need them for it will be the middle of November probably before the marsh is frozen.

We punt in the direction so the ducks will get up on the right hand side. This makes the shooting swing easier. No noise now. Don't shoot if the kill is to fall in some place where it can not be retrieved. We may have good luck and we may not. I may shoot well or

I may have a bad streak when I can not hit a barn. I never know when these bad streaks are to come or what makes them, but all who shoot have these bad days. We hear the noon train pass in the distance. It is lunch time and we may as well rest for two or three hours, so back to the blind, get out the lunch bucket, a smoke, and then a snooze for the afternoon flight doesn't amount to much these still, warm days in October. By and by Herman touches me and whispers, "There are some redheads in the decoys." I take a peek. Sure enough there are half a dozen that have come in unnoticed by either of us. I stand up to give them a chance. Bewildered they do not fly. I shake my gun at them and yell and Hermant throws an empty shell. This starts them and I get the shot of both barrels on the wing. I hear a companion shooting now and then at the far end of the marsh and then a flock of bluebills come from his direction. Maybe I have a shot, maybe I do not, but it is a great day to be alive and out of doors.

It is near the close of day. Open water duck won't pay attention to decoys late in the day. Besides, while the law would let us shoot an hour or two longer and the bag is quite below the legal limit, I have enough. I may take a whack at the coots on my way home. The French fishermen like them better than ducks and in exchange gladly give me perch, herring or walleyes, still kicking fresh from Saginaw Bay.

My companion comes in soon after I reach the boathouse. Our ducks are hung in a cool place. We are at the Tobico Marsh today, not far from the Saginaw River's mouth. Dinner, cigars. The evening is chilly so a fire of white birch in the fireplace is cheering. A game of old sledge or seven up and by nine-thirty in bed.

November is here. Cold and raw, a veritable duck day. A little ice formed around the shore rushes during the night. The wind is from the northwest and blowing great guns. Again the Tobico Marsh. We do not get away until seven o'clock. No hurry, the day will be long enough anyhow. Canvasbacks were here yesterday. Geese have been passing south for a week. The herring gulls are flapping over the open water of the marsh. Scaup and ringbills are more plentiful than they were in October. All the bluewinged teal have gone, but greenwings are a plenty and great greenhead mallards from the far north are here. Wisps of snipe are in the air. "Sawbills" and golden eyes and butterballs too are plentiful. All of this means the end is near. How differently the marsh affects you today than when the opening day was here. The rat houses are completed and stick up from every cove and pond hole. The cattails have largely shed their seed down but now and then a bunch is sent flying by the day's cold wind gust. All is yellow and brown. The forest margin is bare of leaves except the red oaks. The pines and white birches are more prominent. All of the marsh bird life is gone except the waterfowl and now and then a marsh hawk with white rump sailing on unsteady wing close to the grasses looking for a wounded duck, for he has collected many of them this autumn. A crow now and then crosses the marsh to the woodland. It has been feeding on the sands of the bay shore where a clam or dead fish or crab is still to be had.

Picking up decoys now is no fun and what a temptation it is to leave them out until the next day in hopes it will not be so cold on the fingers. We are in luck if the blind proves a good wind break, and we hope we don't have to chase cripples. How the dead grasses bend and billow in the wind. One thinks the marsh on such a day a lonesome place; sort of a haunted house. A grand expanse, no longer a place of dreamy quiet, yet we are full of happiness and satisfaction, for the cause of this absence of quiet is the north wind that makes a real duck day.

Rail Shooting

THE Sora, or Ortolan, that little laughing witch of the marshes, has furnished me with many a day's sport. First of all he is here earlier than the other marsh and bog sorts. While we have a few Wilson's snipe that breed here, there is not much use hunting them until the northern flight comes in, well after the middle of September, but early in September the rail are plentiful. The wild rice is beginning to harden and drop and these little fellows can absorb quantities of this rich and attractive food. It is amazing how much of it they can stuff into their gizzards. Their gizzards are much larger in proportion than any other bird that I know of, and they are crammed jam full of rice; seems as if sometimes I had taken a tablespoonful out of one of these gizzards, for I always clean them and consider them tidbits to go with the birds themselves. The liver too is large and worth saving, and while I am speaking of the cooking end of it, I might just as well finish that part now before I tell of the shooting.

We at home were all very fond of rail. Sometimes they would be spitted on a long skewer, three or four of them, and broiled over the fire, but more often put between a wire broiling iron, a dozen or twenty of them, and quickly toasted over the coals, so that they still were red and juicy when the breasts were cut; amply buttered, with a little bit of currant jelly and piping hot right from the fire, and the old fashioned broiling fire was almost always hickory or its bark. There are only two birds that equal or are better — the jacksnipe and the golden plover. I think the golden plover the best of all the birds that fly, and to my notion the woodcock ranks below any of the three that I have mentioned. Our favorite way of cooking rail was to make a deep pie with a biscuit dough crust, good and thick, and lots of juice or gravy. We picked the birds when we could so as to have the benefit of the flavor of the fat, for they are fat as butter after they have been feeding on the rice a few days, but sometimes this would prove impossible on account of the tender skin. Then the birds were skinned, but ordinarily there were some of them that we could pick so we had a fair amount of the fat for flavoring and juice. Simmered over a slow fire until they were tender, then put in a deep baking pan lined with crust and covered with a crust, a liberal lump of butter, some peppercorns coarsely ground, and then put in the oven and baked to a rich brown, there was nothing ever came on the table more toothsome. "The four and twenty blackbirds baked into a pie" in good King Arthur's time I think must have been rail to have lived so long in history as a toothsome dish.

As to the shooting; I have talked enough about the table. The vast rice fields of the Saginaw River marshes afforded a wonderful feeding ground for thousands, yes and hundreds of thousands, of rail. By the third or fourth of September usually they were plentiful. A slap on the side of the canoe with your paddle would bring forth a derisive laugh or rail from all over the marsh, and the sudden whistle of a mill would start them cackling and tittering and railing for miles around.

The shooting was the same as rail bird shooting everywhere, only we do not have to wait for the tide as they do on the seashore, but the higher the water the easier the pushing through the rice and the more shooting, because the birds flushed easier and did not skulk and run away as readily as when the water was low and the footing and hide better. A North wind raised the water in the Saginaw marshes, so when we had a chance to choose the day, we waited for the north wind, but it made little difference, for the rail were so plentiful we could usually get enough anyhow.

Seated in the bow of the canoe or duck boat with a man in the stern to push at as good a rate of speed as he could through the rice, the birds would flush ahead of the boat and one had a variety of shots, but very few straight ahead, most always to the right or left, the birds making for the fringe and cover of the rice bed margin. It seems to be a favorite trick of the rail to get up just opposite you and fly around you, occasioning a hard twisting shot, and if you were not careful you would be apt to overturn the boat. On the salt water marshes I believe they have boats that are wide enough and steady enough so a man can stand up to do his shooting. That would be a great advantage, but in our marshes the cover was so dense that we had to have very small boats and the shooting had to be done from a sitting position. The punter of course stood up, but he could balance himself with his pole. Otherwise the craft was very tottery, and many a bird I have missed because of the boat giving a sudden twist or turn just as I touched the trigger.

I recall some years ago, before there was a bag limit, I went down to Cheboyganing marshes and in something like four hours' shooting killed sixty-nine rail. A few days later, taking more ammunition, I came home with 110.

It is quite a chore marking them down. I have tried throwing painted blocks as markers for the fallen birds, but this doesn't work very well, and my punter was a good marker with my help. Then again I am careful not to shoot birds that I know we are not going to be able to find.

Of late years rail shooting has been more difficult owing to so much of the marsh being drained, but it is only recently that I recall getting my limit of fifty of the Carolina rail, that being the legal bag, in just two hours' shooting This was after the days of the automobile, quite different from when we used to have to paddle clear down there from Saginaw. My canoe was put bottom upwards, resting on the windshield and the hood, and we sped down the Bay City road to the crossing of Cheboyganing Creek where the canoe was launched with good old Alphonse in the stern. We paddled down past the pump house; then the rice beds began. Nearing the upper railroad bridge we find birds in plenty and before we have gotten to the Interurban Bridge I have my fifty. I began shooting at eleven o'clock and at one had my limit. We paddled down Cheboyganing to Zilwaukee, telephoned for the automobile and were back home at three o'clock.

My gun is an open 16-gauge, 26-inch barrels, which I have spoken of before I think, and for rail shooting I load with two drams of smokeless powder, E. C. or Schultz, and either 7/8 or 3/4 of an ounce of No. 10 shot. One should not shoot more than 7/8 of an ounce of shot in a 16-gauge gun, no matter what the game is.

How glorious are the marshes at rail time. It is your first outing. A mud hen or gallinule skitters away ahead of you; there may still be the chug of an enormous bullfrog; great white lilies in full bloom everywhere. As you paddle along quietly you are startled and give an involuntary jump because of the splurge of an immense carp that has been basking or feeding near the surface,and through the shallow pond holes this commotion of the carp is most active — splurge after splurge until you think the place is full of fish, yet look sharply as you can and rarely can you see one, although you almost run the bow of the canoe onto the fish at times before it makes its splurge. Bitterns and great blue herons get up. Sometimes you will run so close onto a bittern that when it springs into the air with its startled cry, you get another tremor, for your nerves are all on edge expecting something, you don't know what. Now and then a teal or black duck or mallard gets out of the rice and flocks of wood ducks pass by. All the time the rice is dropping into the canoe. The barb on it causes it to crawl, and if you have a crawly shirt on, the first thing you know you have one of these down the back of your neck and you can not shoot or do anything until it is extricated. Don't get one in your throat. If you do, you are liable to go to a doctor to have it out. You hear a train pass over the trestle of the long marsh. Great hawks soar and skirt and plane the marshes; the white spot on the rump tells you it is the marsh hawk. Marsh wrens, blackbirds and various sandpipers are in evidence. Webs of invisible spiders are spun all about the upstanding rushes; a lazy drone of bees and now and then a stinging mosquito, but a great silent place after all; a peaceful, restful place with an odor all its own — an odor that tells you of many happy days with ducks, snipe and now with rail.

We did not do much rail shooting with the old muzzle loading guns. Once in a while a day would be taken for it, but it was not often; it required so much loading and there was usually so much other shooting that was more attractive, for in the early days the duck season opened September first, so by the time the rail were here there was good duck shooting. Then too we had summer woodcock shooting and lots of plover, but of late years there is no other shooting before the sixteenth of September, when the duck season opens, so that rail shooting today fills quite a niche, and takes the place of the snipe, plover, woodcock and early duck shooting of old.

Once in a while we used to get king rail in the Saginaw marshes, but they never were very plentiful. The Virginia rail we find breeding here in Michigan but in the out of way, isolated spots — the small bog holes or little marshes of the woodlands. I never have seen them on the big river marshes.

THE NICHOLS DEER HUNTING CAMP ON THE AU SABLE RIVER IN 1876

From left to right: Samuel J. Tilus, David Shepard, Billy Simpson, John Nichols, Edwin C. Nichols, Cornelius Aultman, Canton, Ohio, Rev. Reed Stuart and John T. Nichols

A Sketch of the

Nichols Deer Hunting Camps

Contributed by Edwin C. Nichols
Battle Creek, Michigan

THE State of Michigan, especially the Lower Peninsula, was in the early days a veritable hunter's paradise. Perhaps no other section of the country of equal dimensions carried such an amount and variety of game and fish as did Michigan, the surrounding big lakes furnishing immense quantities of the finest food fish in the world, while the interior lakes with which the state is dotted, comprising lakes from a few acres in extent up to thirty square miles, with numerous incoming and outgoing streams of most beautiful water, were extremely favorable for the propagation and growth of smaller fish, including the fontinalis or speckled trout, all varieties of bass, perch, blue gills, pan fish not excelled in any of the fish markets of the world. Several streams also were peopled by the grayling, a rare fish then unknown outside of some portions of Great Britain and Europe.

In addition to all this, the woods and forests were the habitat of a wonderful variety of game animals, of which the deer was prominent, as the country was very favorable for its growth — the margin of the streams and forests generally furnishing protection and above all, abundant food. There was also a great number of the smaller furred animals, including the beaver, mink, otter and muskrat. The lordly wild turkey was a native found in large numbers. Old Bruin, the black bear, was frequently seen, and an occasional wolf, bob cat and swamp lynx added zest to the hunt.

It was into this beautiful and productive country that my father, Mr. John Nichols, came with his little family to Battle Creek, Calhoun County, Michigan, in the spring of 1848. He started in business there by building a small foundry and machine shop, being almost the first one in southern Michigan. Although he was, as Saint Paul admonishes, very "diligent in business," he was also a great lover of nature, of the forest and streams, of the flora and all wild life. He enjoyed in good measure the out of doors life which his love of nature and sports brought to him.

One of his business ethics was to take a few weeks each year for what he called his deer hunting and nature outing camp. This camp in the early days was an unpretentious affair compared with its somewhat luxurious development in later days. The usual procedure then was to hitch a pair of good horses to a big lumber wagon in which was placed a heavy canvas tent, some suitable blankets, a supply of tin table china, very primitive cooking utensils including of course the coffee and tea pots, plenty of salt pork and a bag of those home-made doughnuts, a small supply of groceries, to all of which was to be added the choicest selection of deer meat, game birds and excellent fish. The latter were to be obtained at will on short notice at the very threshold of the camp. There was never lack of grand food and plenty of it.

Under this shelter and amid these attractive surroundings would come the little band of happy hunters, each armed with a muzzel loading rifle, down which the powder and ball were pushed with a long ramrod, and carefully primed with a percussion cap. For this was the day before the invention of the murderous repeating rifle with its magazine of cartridges, enabling the shooter to pour a volley on the poor deer without much regard to skill or marksmanship. The olden hunter had his single barrelled muzzle loading rifle, giving him but one shot and one chance at the deer, and thus requiring on his part steady nerve, accurate eye and delicate trigger finger to make this one chance a killing one. It was indeed a good sporting accomplishment to place this one little rifle ball in a vital part of a running deer, of which the modern hunter with his magazine rifle knows nothing. The imaginative lover of these goodly scenes who has enjoyed, as some of us have, these wonderful surroundings would not willingly lose the memory of those happy and thrilling events.

The party usually carried one and sometimes two deer hounds mainly for tracking wounded deer, but occasionally to make a drive in the early morning to stir them up a little. Any true sportsman who has on a keen, frosty, early morning listened to the music of one or two loud baying hounds following the wily buck in full swing will not soon forget the electric thrill that the chase brings to every hunter within hearing; each hoping the deer is headed for his stand and with every sense acute, every muscle tense, he listens to the echoes and re-echoes of the baying dogs as it follows on the track of the flying deer.

Thus it was, that year by year the Nichols Deer Hunting Camps were located for several weeks each season in various parts of the Lower Peninsula of Michigan. The outfit gradually increased in its hospitable features until there was a large cooking and dining tent with a good wooden floor, capacious table with its white tablecloth and napkins and a fine show of modern chinaware and table silver, comfortable chairs, a large cooking stove with hot water reservoir, and an especially large pancake griddle, capacious sleeping tents with comfortable bedding, a commissary tent for the storage of provisions with auxiliary tents for extra guests or other purposes, so that it was not uncommon to have a hunting party of twenty persons, all invited guests, and the hunt frequently lasted thirty to forty days.

The hunting ground gradually moved farther and farther away from the home town, and the importance of these annual hunts and the hospitality of its founder became quite well heralded throughout the country. The hunting grounds chosen in the earlier years were in many counties of the Lower Peninsula such as Barry, Allegan, Muskegon, Montcalm, Isabella, Gratiot and others. Notwithstanding the great increase in cultivated land and the cutting away of the forests, there still remained large areas of good deer hunting ground in the lower part of the peninsular state.

I recall with pleasure that in the year 1870, one of the hunting camps was in Gratiot County, to which we proceeded by lumber wagons, going through the town of Ovid and finding our camp ground only a few miles from that thriving little village. It was here that some of our party coming into camp one day following an old corduroy road through a forbidding swamp, came upon a native, driving a pair of rather poor looking horses, patched up harness and an old lumber wagon without a box, but instead with a couple of heavy planks serving as a platform, on which the native was seated carrying a few bags of meal, potatoes and other necessary food and fodder. He was a goodly specimen of a hardy handed pioneer, not overly clothed, and the whole outfit looking pretty forlorn. Of course we treated him with all the hospitality of our vocations as hunters and friendly strangers, he being offered free access to our drinking flasks to which he took with genuine avidity. After being fully warmed up and cared for in the line of refreshments and smokes, we were entertained by his friendly gossip concerning the neighborhood, which was mostly about the local hunting, fishing and timbering. As we were leaving, one of our party remarked to him that things did not seem very prosperous just in that vicinity, to which with a rare twinkle in his eye, he responded,

"Well now, stranger, I ain't nigh so poor as you might think, for I don't own a foot of land around here." Not long since, the writer had the pleasure of driving through this same locality in an automobile and witnessing the beautiful farms, splendid farm buildings and all the evidence of rural wealth and prosperity to be found in any fertile and well cultivated land. The memory of this scene came back to him and he wondered if and hoped that our native friend had really later in life come into possession of some of that very same land. This Gratiot County hunt yielded a goodly number of deer and plenty of small game and in addition Mr. Cornelius Aultman of Canton, Ohio, shot and killed the largest black bear that our party ever met.

One of the most interesting of the Nichols Hunting Camps was on the Au Sable River in the fall of 1876, when the party were taken by rail to Roscommon and then down the South Branch of the river. This party of hunters, with its extensive equipment and all needful provisions for a six weeks sojourn in this beautiful wilderness, together with ten thoroughbred deer hounds, was loaded into five big scow boats which were prepared and transported there for the purpose, and they went gaily sailing down that beautiful stream on a bright October day. The South Branch at that time was densely wooded with overhanging trees along the margin, and grand strips of Norway and white pine bordering it. It was a fine rushing torrent down which the boats sped with little effort except to dodge the overhanging sweepers and clear the treacherous whirlpools. A temporary camp was made before reaching the junction of the main stream of the Au Sable.

On the following day the permanent camp was located a few miles below the junction near what was then known as Ball's bridge. The picture facing page No. 89 shows one portion of this camp, while there was another detachment a short distance below. The Au Sable River at this point was then well filled with grayling, a rare sporting fish of the brook trout type with all its beauty of colors and gameness in action. It was here that one day in a slight snow storm, I saw Mr. Albert A. Sprague of Chicago, Illinois, with his five ounce fly rod take from its water a goodly number of these beautiful grayling, a splendid game fish and the first of its kind I had ever seen. The grayling has since entirely disappeared from the Au Sable waters, but it will always be remembered as a glorious game fish by those who were so fortunate as to make its acquaintance. This camp had every attraction of location and surroundings and with abundance of game and fish and the fine companionship of the goodly family gathered on its shores, it will always remain a most cherished memory.

Our favorite hunting camp site and one which we occupied for several successive years was on the north bank of the river a few miles below where the North Branch joins its rushing waters with the majestic main stream of the Au Sable. It was a beautiful hillside crowned with a grove of stately Norway pines, sloping gently down to the water's edge, forming a delightful frontage looking up stream.

A brook of fine spring water found its gurgling way to the river at this point. On exploring this brook, we found it was the home of a fine colony of beavers who had built across it a wonderful dam, showing almost human reasoning and judgment in the selection of the site and in the engineering skill required in its construction. This dam caused a water pond of considerable depth and of many acres in extent, in the midst of which were two well constructed houses or homes for the beavers. The beaver family were there in goodly numbers and all about were to be found evidences of their skill and laborious workmanship in the cutting of trees, some of them eight inches in diameter, with several canals leading inward to enable the cuttings to be transported homeward. We treated this interesting family with such friendliness that they soon grew to know us as good neighbors and went on with their regular workings without much hesitation. It was with deep regret that on one of our seasonal visits to this camp, we found the commercial trapper had opened the dam and doubtless taken possession of most of the occupants.

When our "Tented City" was in full regalia on this beautiful hillside, it presented a very interesting and charming picture as one rounded the river bend above and came into full view.

Thus these annual Nichols Deer Hunts continued for many years, mostly on the Au Sable River and its tributaries, finally reaching into the Upper Peninsula going into the counties of Delta, Marquette, and Dickinson. Facing page No. 98 is a picture of one of the camps in Dickinson County in '86, quite descriptive of the general features of such a forest home and suggesting to the sympathetic and experienced sportsman the many pleasures and comforts to be found in such a camp.

When the time came that it was unlawful to use dogs for hunting deer, the Nichols Hunting Camp was formally suspended. The party saw no real pleasure or true sport in the mere potting or killing of deer by the hunter who sits shivering on the runway and waits for the poor deer to show himself within range of the murderous repeater, which gives the deer but little chance, while it contributes considerable danger to the surrounding neighborhood. The rifles were hung up, the camp equipage stored away, but the memory of those happy days is still gratefully and lovingly cherished by the few of us who still remain.

The Michigan Sportsman's Association

THE above association was organized in 1875. Its first officers were:

President—Robt. P Toms, Detroit.
1st Vice-President—E. S. Holmes, Grand Rapids.
2nd Vice-President—D. H. Fitzhugh, Jr., BayCity.
Secretary—Edw. Weeks, Mt. Clemens.
Treasurer—C. C. Cadman, Detroit.

In 1876 Dr. E. S. Holmes of Grand Rapids was elected President and he held that office until 1883 and probably longer, as I have not the records of the association beyond that date. In 1881 I was elected Secretary and held that office for a number of years.

This organization had a great deal to do with the framing of the game laws in the early days and the establishment of a game warden system. It was composed of old time sportsmen, quite different from the present generation.

The proceedings, printed in book form, are in my possession for the five years beginning 1878 and ending with 1882, and they are filled with addresses or papers prepared by ornithologists and fish culturists and teem with scientific and technical lore. One can not read their pages without being impressed with the earnest

THE NICHOLS DEER HUNTING CAMP ON THE STURGEON RIVER, DICKINSON COUNTY, UPPER PENINSULA, MICHIGAN, 1886

effort that was made in that early day to save our wild life of forest and stream, marsh and lake. The quotations that I have made from these printed proceedings are fit evidence of the character of the old time sportsmen.

EXTRACT FROM A PAPER READ BEFORE THE MICHIGAN SPORTSMAN'S ASSOCIATION AT LANSING, JANUARY 26TH, 1881, BY H. B. RONEY, EAST SAGINAW, MICHIGAN

This was reproduced in pamphlet form and a copy of same is in my possession. The writer made a thorough investigation of the slaughter of deer for the year 1880 and submits a table showing the number of deer shipped from the stations of the old Jackson, Lansing & Saginaw Railroad beginning at Gaylord on the north and ending with Pinconning on the south, to have been 10,000 deer.

Just think of it, you who read today, that in that year from the station of Pinconning, only twenty miles from Bay City, there were 12,500 lbs. of venison shipped; from Standish, the next station, less than forty miles, there was 90,000 lbs.; 150,000 lbs from Summit; 187,500 lbs from West Branch, and Roscommon tops the list with 250,000 lbs. Then north of there the quantity gradually subsides until we reach Gaylord, which shipped about 12,500 lbs.

The deer surely worked northward. There were not nearly as many deer in the woods of the Turtle Lake Club, which is thirty miles south and west of

Alpena, thirty-five years ago when the land was first acquired as there are at the present time; but returning to Mr. Roney's article I quote from one of the closing paragraphs:

"TOTAL EXTINCTION INEVITABLE"

"These statistics give a grand total of 70,000 deer, or about 10,000,000 pounds of venison destroyed in Michigan in the one year of 1880. At this rate how long will it take to exterminate the species in Michigan? How long can the state stand this drain, before the last relic of the noble race disappears? Just about five years, and they will become scarce in less than twelve months, as indeed they are already. And when the present supply is gone, where can the next come from? Certainly not from the north, east or west, for that is a geographical impossibility, while from the south it can not be expected. Unlike other states which border upon vast wildernesses out of which a new supply comes to replenish the disappearing race, the Lower Peninsula of Michigan, when it has once permitted this noble animal to be exterminated between Lakes Michigan and Huron, has forever lost a great source of wealth and valuable food supply, which if now wisely preserved will last for generations.

"The immense increase from 21,000 deer destroyed in 1878 to 70,000 in 1880, is due in part to the cold weather which came early and continued steadily throughout the fall, which permitted safe shipment, but principally to the prohibitory export laws of surrounding states, which are driving into Michigan all the professional market hunters in the country. Can a legislature which is cognizant of these facts, delay longer that self protection which is the first law of nature, as it is of states and of nations?

"The Remedy"

"Of the 70,000 deer killed in Michigan in 1880, about 50,000 were shipped from the state or destroyed for the hides. The remedy is plain. Declare the killing of game for other purposes than consumption as food within this state illegal, as recommended by our 'Committee on laws for the protection of game animals of fur and feather and insectivorous birds.' Then all game shipped from the state will be prima facie killed in violation of the law. This will save 30,000 to 32,000 deer yearly. Then declare it a crime to kill deer in the red or spotted coat, or have in possession such red or spotted coat hides, and the killing for hides will almost wholly cease, and illegal killing for lumber camps will be greatly restricted, saving 15,000 to 20,000 more deer yearly, and reducing the annual holocaust from 70,000 to about 15,000 or 18,000.

"Then totally prohibit the killing of deer while in the water and this will save say 1,000 more, as it will in a measure restrict the practice of 'shining.' As the Michigan Sportsman's Association has unanimously recommended the total prohibition of killing in water, and the same is likely to become a law, this fact must effectually silence those who oppose dogs because they drive the deer to water. With these amendments made, there will be game enough in this state for the uses of all its citizens for all time to come."

Then follows a document as to whether a non-export law would be unconstitutional, and numerous court decisions are cited.

AT THE PORTABLE HOUSE

(1907)

Clark Ring with violin. *From left to right,* W. A. Avery, George B. Morley, C. H. Davis, Jack Morley (always the best dancer) in the center, G. D. Seib, E. N. Briggs. *In rear,* Marden, the cook, and Geo. Gale, the chore boy.

Hunting and Camping Trips with Jack Morley

ONE of my early shooting companions was Jack Morley. Jack came to Saginaw from the "wild and woolly west" — Fort Scott, Kansas. He was about my age, or a year or two older, a short, sawed-off individual, but everyone said Jack was the best company in the world. He could see something funny about everything and his descriptive powers were wonderful. He could embellish and make a good story out of almost nothing.

About the first I recall of our camping trips was when Jack and I pooled about $25.00 or $30.00 (that was a lot of money those days and we looked upon it as an enormous investment) and with it bought a tent, a little sheet iron stove and a double cot. This cot was a wonder, a cross legged affair with a bar running down the middle which left a baggy, saggy, canvas so-called "resting place" either side of this bar. Jack complained that I was restless and rolling over always pulled the blankets off him. On one trip he nailed my good California blankets to the side of the cot with ten-penny nails using an axe for the purpose and that edge of the blankets ever after looked as if it had been scalloped and made into drawnwork.

We used to either take our outfit out six or ten miles

by team and camp for two or three days partridge shooting, or we shipped it out on the narrow gauge road to Unionville, Kintner, or some of those places and got a farmer to draw it to destination for us, but we never went very far away.

Jack was easily lost. You could put him in a ten acre lot and in fifteen minutes he would not know which way to get out. That reminds me of our trip north of Freeland. We took Briggs with us that time, my good old friend E. N. Briggs, one of the nicest men I ever knew and one of the best shots. Briggs had a Gordon setter by the name of Mose I had given to him and Dick Carter had broken him. I had old Bob at the time. We started the team from the mill very early in the morning for the camping place. I don't know how we ever directed the teamster but we did have an understanding as to just the spot, and as he took a man along to help him, they put the tent up, fixed the camp for us and drove back to Saginaw, a pretty good day's work. It is eleven miles from Saginaw to Freeland and we were north of Freeland. We took the afternoon train which left Saginaw in those days at four o'clock and got a farmer to drive us to camp. Undoubtedly these things were arranged beforehand for that time of the year, it was the fore part of December, it gets dark pretty early. I always did the cooking and Jack was mighty handy at dish washing and we let Briggs do the tidying up around camp. He was neater than either Jack or I and he tended the fire and helped get up wood and water. Well, we had a nice, comfortable tent, one cot on one side for Briggs and the double cot on the other side for Jack and myself, and a few boards laid in between made sufficient floor. Then there was the little stove just at the foot of Briggs' bed. I had fetched along some cannel coal thinking it would keep the fire during the night and be easier than firing with wood. It didn't take a great while to get settled. I cooked a good supper. It was very cold, and the dogs were given a good comfortable place within the tent and we went to bed early.

Before going to bed Jack asked, "Whereabouts are we? What section are we on? You know I always get lost and I want to know so that I can ask a farmer if I see one and tell him where our camp is." "Well, Jack, we are located on the northeast quarter of the northeast quarter of section 37," I answered. "All you have to do if you get lost is have some farmer tell you where section 37 is and you can find your way back." Briggs confirmed this, and it never occurred to us that Jack did not get on to it that we were joking and that there are only thirty-six sections in a township.

We went to bed having first put a good chunk of that quick burning coal in the stove, for it was a mighty cold night and would be down to below zero before morning. Pretty soon the coal got to going and you could hear the little stove roaring. Then the stove pipe began to get red and it got redder and redder until Briggs thought it was dangerously near conflagration, jumped out of bed, put a cup of water on the coal and shut the draft. We went to sleep and in the course of an hour or two we were all cold. Briggs got up and opened the draft, went back to bed and the tent soon warmed up again. Pretty soon we could hear it roar and the same old cherry red was creeping gradually towards the tent top when out of bed rolled Briggs again, shut the draft and watered the coal. This performance he repeated several times during the night, while Jack and I in our double cot passed the night in comfort.

The others were not as early risers as I. After making the fire in the morning I took the gun and slipped out to see if I could not find some partridges budding, for in those days we did not think it much of a crime to shoot a partridge out of a tree. The hardwood trees were going off like pistol shots, the cold was so intense. My breath was frosty and white frost hung to all of the bushes. I hadn't gone far before I saw partridges in the trees scattered around and I shot three or four, not all of them out of the trees, however, for some of them would skyrocket away at my approach and once in a while I made a difficult shot. I came back and by that time the others were up.

When Jack saw the string of birds he wanted to go and do likewise. I warned him I was going to get breakfast at once, that I would have it ready in half an hour and for him not to go far, which he promised. I made the coffee, had a good big frying pan full of raw fried potatoes, cooked the sausage and went to the door to look for Jack, and called to him. I had heard him shoot two or three times and the last shot seemed to be quite a way off. We waited as long as we could and he didn't appear, so Briggs and I had our breakfast and wondered what had become of him. We knew he was lost but we didn't know what the outcome would be. After an hour or so he showed up, quite used up, and looking about as near mad as he ever could be. His first words were, "I thought you said our camp was on section 37; it is no such thing; he says this is section 28."

Well, we let him tell his story. It seems he had become lost as usual. He finally came out to a road, went down the road and met a farmer. He stopped and asked the farmer where section 37 was and the farmer asked him "what kind of a damned fool he thought he was, and what he was trying to do, string him?" Jack said, "He came near licking me, but I finally convinced him that I was honest about it and I was looking for camp. 'Well,' he says, 'if you're the fellows that came in here and put up that tent yesterday, they are over there in section 28. Go down to the corner and go north and you will see it.' 'But,' I said, 'I don't know which way north is from south; you point the direction,' which he did, and he asked me, 'Who said you were on section 37?' and I said, 'Mr. Mershon.' He looked kind of funny at that and laughed. Were you fellows stringing me or what was he laughing at?" For a long while after that Jack was known as "Old Section 37."

I recall we had a very good day's shooting after all. We got a late start. Pretty soon the sun came out and while it was cold it turned out to be a very good day. We hunted quite a while before finding anything. Finally just as we were getting over a fence alongside a poplar thicket by a sand ridge we sat and rested on the top rail for a while and Jack called my attention to Bob on a point. We got over there and a partridge got up which we killed, and we had point after point, for it was quite open, until we had killed eight or ten birds. The place seemed full of them.

Another camping trip I recall was out north of Fairgrove. We put up a pretty good camp here, for we had invited a number of guests to go with us, among them Ferd Ashley and Ed McCarty, two fat men weighing about 240 pounds each. I know that because I had picked out my place in the camp bed and slept between them because I thought they would keep me warm, but they stuck up in the air so high that the blankets did not touch me and there I was in a vacant space without a bit of bedding anywhere near me. We had been there a day or two and George Morley joined us and a friend of mine from Morristown, N. J., a lumberman who always wanted to go on one of our shooting trips. He was poorly equipped, for he had patent leather shoes and there was some snow on the ground. I made a big rabbit stew the first night and McCarty, as well as the others, ate heartily of it, but it did not affect all of them the same as it did Mac, for he was made very sick and the effect was similar to sea sickness. My New Jersey friend's thin socks were put on sticks to dry near the place that McCarty had selected for the rail of his ship. The next morning two farmers came to call on us. We heard them as they came near the campfire. We were not out of bed yet. One of them said to the other, "Well, I have heard of a fellow throwing up his socks before, but I never saw it, but here they are." We had to furnish New Jersey with new socks for his day's hunting.

He went with me that day and after we had had a satisfactory tramp and shooting of partridges we came across the tracks of some wild turkeys. The snow was very thin and after following them sometime we lost them entirely, for the snow was gone. We both regretted this very much, but the New Jersey man probably more than I, for his heart was set on having a wild turkey to take home with him. He became tired along early in the afternoon and I put him on the road to camp and said I would hunt a couple of hours longer, hoping possibly to run on to the tracks. I did not do this, but came out on a cross road and in a farmer's yard was a beautiful flock of bronze tame turkeys. I made a bargain with the farmer's wife to let me shoot one of them. I paid her and picking out a ten or twelve pound bird that most resembled a wild turkey, shot it, slung it over my shoulder and tramped into camp and presented it to my New Jersey friend as a wild turkey. It was a long while after that before anyone knew the difference. He wrote me and said his wife thought it was the finest turkey she had ever eaten, far superior to any tame turkey and so different; it had such a sweet, gamey flavor.

Our bag generally was a mixed one. Rabbits were rarely ever brought home, but sometimes cooked in camp. There were always quail to sweeten the bag, but the main dependence was the partridge or ruffed grouse.

Once when we were shy of soap for washing the dishes, Jack got hold of a cake of my Cashmere Bouquet, a very highly scented soap. I didn't know what he was at until I came to use the dishes afterwards. We had only tin plates, and a tin plate smeared with Cashmere Bouquet soap is surely an odorous article.

Once Jack and I took a trip to Unionville on the S. T. & H. Railway. We were after ducks. That has always been known as the "crock of butter trip." We borrowed a little stove of the hardware man. I had a small duck boat and tent. There was a little island somewhere not far from shore there at Unionville, for the drive to Saginaw Bay from the railroad was only two or three miles, maybe not as far as that. It is a long while ago and I have forgotten. We were told that around this little island we would get good duck shooting. After the farmer had deposited the boat on the shore, we loaded it; put in the stove and all of our stuff and the tent poles. They were longer than the boat and stuck out diagonally, and they proved our undoing. There was a choppy sea, but it didn't amount to much and I had no doubt but that we could cross to the island with perfect safety. Jack was in the bow and I was standing up in the stern poling the boat.

Jack had expressed some apprehension, but I told him to "fear not but trust in Dollinger; watch your Uncle do it." One of the choppy seas gave the boat a twist and the tent poles caught the next wave. You take a diagonal tent pole sticking out and jamming into every wave and a duck boat immediately becomes an uncertain animal. Overboard we went quicker than a flash. The water was cold, but it wasn't deep, so we had no difficulty in fishing the stuff from the bottom and loading up and getting in, but I didn't stand up that time and I was more careful. By the time we reached the island it was blowing pretty hard. We rigged up our tent the best we could and that night the wind howled so I thought it would blow the island and all out into Saginaw Bay. There wasn't a duck to be seen. We couldn't find one anywhere around the island or in the marsh, and when the storm lulled the next afternoon we got across to the mainland to go home, first buying from a farmer a crock of butter. When G. W. Morley, Jack's uncle, asked what luck we had duck shooting, Jack was quite shy, but had a good deal to say about what a beautiful crock of butter we got, and ever after that the boys dubbed this duck hunting expedition of ours the "crock of butter trip"—and years afterwards when a hunt resulted in a failure or the bag was slim, it was alluded to as a "crock of butter" trip.

The Old Hunting Car

IN 1883 Coups Circus got into difficulties and its advertising car was sold at sheriff's sale at Saginaw. This was bought by the Wells-Stone deer hunting party. There were some outsiders taken in on this venture. I don't know how many stockholders there were originally, possibly twenty. The car was remodelled and made into a hunting car. There were six lower berths, six upper berths, a kitchen at one end and an observation room or dining room in the other, a large ice box, storage room and all that sort of thing. It was finished in plain white ash. The work was done at the Pere Marquette car shops. It would have been considered a very crude affair in later days, but it was a thing of joy. It was used for several years for deer hunting — a camp on wheels. Deer were near Saginaw then — up to the Oxbow, over around Harrison or Clare.

In 1883 the car was filled jam full to go to Yellowstone Park. It was attached to the train that followed the Villard-Hatch party when they went to drive the golden spike that connected the eastern and western ends of the Northern Pacific. This was in September of 1883. My father was one of the party, and it was the last trip that he ever took, for he died the following spring. We did a little duck shooting on the way out. We stopped at New Buffalo, N. D. Mr.

HUNTING CAR "CITY OF SAGINAW"

Return from Dawson, N. D., 1889

This now looks like game hog picture, but it was quite the correct thing in the old days to be proud of big bag, but this represented the game brought home by party of nine for two weeks hunting trip when it was legal to bring your game home and there was no bag limit or any idea of growing scarcity.

There has been great change in the last fifteen or twenty years and pictures of dead game are instantly branded game hog pictures

Goodsell from Grand Rapids had a ranch a few miles north and there were sloughs around that ranch that were filled with ducks. Up to that time I never had seen as many ducks as I saw on those sloughs. In going through Dawson we were told what a wonderful place it was for all kinds of waterfowl, especially geese.

At Livingstone the Jerome Marble party in the private car "Yellowstone" were sidetracked. They had been in the moutains hunting and had elk, deer, antelope and buffalo meat. My father was an expert angler. We had excellent luck with cutthroat trout, so sociably we traded trout for buffalo meat to the joy of both parties.

In going through the park, and it was all travelled by horseback then, we had an encounter with horse thieves and I was held up by four ruffians, but looked as tough as they did and I got the drop on one of them before he did on me, and the affair passed off bloodlessly. We were fed on elk at one or two places, and at Yancy's were served with buffalo meat.

For a number of years the Saginaw crowd used the car for western trips, for after a while the deer hunters got tired of it and a few of us were able to buy it for a song, so that by the late 80's we were going to Dawson regularly with this car, never less than eight, sometimes ten. The railroads were lenient and generous in those days, and it was far cheaper for us to travel in this way, taking along our own cook and porter and provisions, than it would have been to have gone without the car.

In 1894 we built a new car and formed the Forest and Stream Co., Ltd., consisting of ten members. The car was built by Barney & Smith of Dayton, Ohio, and cost us about $8,000. It was perfectly plain, but it was a larger, stronger car; six wheel trucks; more convenient and roomy. We had the luxury of a bath room with tub. Could carry 500 gallons of water and there was room for about 750 pounds of ice, so that we were quite independent when sidetracked for some time in places where we could not get a good water supply.

We used this car to go to Dawson every October until the goose hunting failed there, and after that when in 1900 we changed to Pleasant Lake, N. D. and the Moose Jaw district of Saskatchewan, the car was used until 1914. After we had the portable house we used to sidetrack the car at Tuxford and drive six or eight miles to begin our housekeeping at Buffalo Lake.

This car was used, too, for hunting parties here in Michigan. We regularly in November put the car in commission for two weeks or longer, sidetracked it at some of the little nearby towns for partridge shooting, and members of the party came and went as suited their convenience. We also used it regularly in May for our trips to the North Branch of the Au Sable for trout fishing, and two or three times had it sidetracked at the end of the Cleveland branch of the D. & M. Railway where it crossed the Black River, or we went in on some one of the logging roads of the Michigan Central where the Black was of easy access.

The car was a great comfort in many ways for with

ample ice and storage facilities we could take care of our game and fish; we had our meals as we wanted them, and some sort of a card game every evening. Those were great old days — the days of the hunting car. It has not been in use now for several years, but has recently been sold to a mining company in the southwest.

Hunting at Dawson, N. D.

THE following, entitled "A Ten Days Trip to Dakota," was written by me at the time; at any rate, I have found it among my old hunting records. It ended abruptly, as you will see, and it was not completed until 1907. I am not reproducing it because of literary merit by any means, but it teems with the enthusiasm of youth. Later on when we were going to Dakota regularly we became familiar with many of the things that were so delightful because of their being new and the first time.

We used to get tremendous bags of geese. The plan was to drive through the stubble fields early in the morning and find where the geese were feeding, make an examination of the ground after the geese had left and see if there was much food left, or if they had been feeding there long, which could be told by the droppings or feathers, and if we had good reason to believe it was a regular feeding, we put in pits. These were holes in the ground between four and five feet in depth and about thirty inches in diameter. The earth was spread out so as to not make much of a mound around the pit and then we plucked or pulled stubble in bunches that we replanted in rows so that the ground would look to have been undisturbed and the stubble would look as if it had originally grown there. If there were two or more of us shooting, we arranged our pits in a

DIGGING GOOSE HOLES NEAR DAWSON, N. D.

October, 1893

row six or eight feet apart. The man in the center acted as Captain and gave the word; the rest were supposed to keep down and not move. The geese fed twice a day. They came into the stubble at daylight and fed until ten or eleven o'clock and then returned to the lake. They came in again between three and four o'clock and fed until dark. On bright still days they flew high and came in later in the afternoon; on stormy days they came in low and began flying earlier, in fact, I have known them to fly all day. Metal profile decoys were used, and it was no uncommon thing for us to kill fifty or sixty geese in one afternoon's or morning's shoot.

The biggest shoot we ever had was sometime in the early 80's on the Troy farm near Tappan, the station just east of Dawson on the Northern Pacific. It was a stormy day; snow squalls all day long. The field we located in was a mile square of wheat stubble. Our party of five divided, three in one part of the field and two in the other. The geese were flying all day, thousands upon thousands of them. We killed 163 that day. We had a farm wagon with extra side boards for carrying eighty bushels of wheat. Our kill nearly filled that wagon box. I know that night when we drove back to Dawson, which I think was eight miles distant, we were cold and wet and we all stuck our legs down in the geese and the warmth of their bodies kept us comfortable. We frequently brought home three hundred or more geese with us, and the arrival of the car in Saginaw was know in advance and our friends by the score flocked to the car to share in our bag. Not a bird was ever wasted, and these wheat fed young geese were very highly considered for the table.

With the goose shooting we had good duck shooting. Lakes Isabelle, Etta and Sibley literally swarmed with all kinds of wild fowl. Every tree claim and sand hill were full of sharptailed grouse. Bag limits and non-shipping out of the state in those days were unknown.

A Ten Days' Trip to Dakota

In September '83, on my return from the Yellowstone Park, I, with a few friends, stopped for two days in eastern Dakota to shoot ducks, and having such fine sport we then and there determined to come again the next year. The best of resolves are more often broken than kept, and when the time came this fall for carrying out the idea, I could not get a party large enough to enable us to take our good hunting car "City of Saginaw." This to me was a great disappointment as there is so much comfort to be had in going in your own car, having your own cook, and as our car is fitted with large ice boxes, we are enabled to save our game to bring home for our friends.

However, on October tenth we left here, three besides myself, and in Chicago were joined my Bob L. of New York and Fred Lord of the Northern Pacific R. R., the latter having business north and spent a day or two with us.

Monday morning found us at Moorhead, Minn. Standing on the rear platform we could count dozens of flocks of geese, hundreds of ducks, snipe and curlew, and every little way a flock of "chickens" would go booming over the prairie. We breakfasted at Fargo just over the line in Dakota, and at ten o'clock stopped with our friend Goodsell at Buffalo. He was expecting us but did not give very encouraging accounts of game; the weather had been so fine that the ducks and geese were still north. Mr. Goodsell has five Canada geese that he caught when young, and by keeping their wings clipped, keeps them tame. Great wild looking fellows they are and whenever a flock of their relatives comes in sight, they set up such a honking that renders the wild ones very uncertain and they often circle around and around the barnyard, almost alighting.

After dinner we loaded ourselves, traps and dogs into wagons and set out for the ranch twelve miles distant. As we drove over the wheat stubbles great flocks of sandhill cranes would take wing just before we would get near enough to shoot. Once this did not prove the case and Charlie blazed away, killing a great big fellow just as he had gotten well under motion; his head and legs dropped and with wings outstretched slowly circled down in a most ludicrous way, but the best he could do, poor fellow. We were all delighted, of course, and as the crane was very fat, visions of a roast floated before our eyes, only dispelled by Mr. Charles saying he was going to express it home to the taxidermist. We found out afterwards he was given to these freaks. For two days did he lug his specimen around and finally he forgot it; left it one night at the depot on the platform, and I saw it going off under a chap's arm early next morning. I said nothing, as it would do someone some good probably.

But to resume: We arrived at the ranch about three o'clock and after making an engagement for supper we spread out along the sloughs. I saw at once our shooting would be poor, for where the year before I had found ponds black with ducks, now only a flock or two were to be seen. The banging of the guns soon started the birds and we had fun enough for the first night. Early next morning we tried it again and by noon were ready for a change, only having bagged eighty-four ducks and four geese, beside a very few snipe. We held a council of war and determined to pull up stakes and make for a place farther west that we had heard great reports from. We got into Buffalo just in time to take the train and arrived Thursday morning on our hunting ground, some 250 miles farther west. Here we had all the shooting we wanted, as you shall see.

Our first concern was to secure means of transportation to and from our shooting grounds, so Bob and I were appointed a committee on transportation and proceeded to interview the livery man. Like a great many of his class, he sized us up for our pile; wanted $8.00 per day for a rig that would carry but three, and said we must pay extra for bringing in our geese. Now the latter part sounded well because it looked like game, but we did not propose to pay some $16.00 or $20.00 per day for riding six or eight miles; that is as we hoped to stay several days, but Mr. Livery Man thought he had us and would not come down a cent. Inwardly wishing him a reserved seat in the place Bob Ingersoll says does not exist, we set about another scheme, and soon we had arranged with a fellow by the name of Long who had a good outfit that would carry our entire party at a reasonable figure. And I will say that Long proved to be a treasure. Little at a time we learned his history, though a very small portion of it I am sure. Educated at one of our eastern colleges, for some reason or other he had gone west soon after graduating. All alone he had trapped the winter before on some Indian Reservation where he had no business to, and had lost all his traps, pelts and outfit; he had been to Jimtown to refit and was now on his way back to some point on the northern Missouri River, way above Bismarck. A mule team, three year old colt and puppy were his only companions. At night he would spread his blankets under the wagon and sleep the sleep of the just; he called it putting up at the "Globe Hotel."

As Bob was bent on duck shooting and the rest of us hankered for geese, we divided; that is, Bob divided; took a buggy and set out for the sloughs four miles south of the track. We piled into Long's wagon and went in the opposite direction. We soon came to a large stubble and it was covered with geese, some feeding but most of them with necks stretched up a yard or two looking at us. Some were for getting out at once and trying to get a shot, but the old head of the party having been there before, said "No." Not one was disturbed but turning to the right we drove on to the large Alkali Lake a few miles further on, here unhitching the team; some loafing, others strolled around the shores of the lake. Ducks and geese covered the surface. I had never seen such clouds of water fowl. When taking wing the roar was like thunder; they would circle around and gradually settle down in another part of the lake. Occasionally we shot a goose or a duck and I got two birds that I set down as avocets. They stood about twelve or thirteen inches high; were white below and gray and black above, and the bills curved upward, being over two inches long, I should judge; I took no measurements, or if I did, I have forgotten them now. I tried to save the skins, but with my usual luck, spoiled them.

About noon the geese began to come in from the stubble and after the first flock they came in a steady stream, alighting far out in the lake. The din was deafening as each flock was welcomed by those already there. Hastily eating our lunch, traps are loaded into the wagon and back we go to the stubble where they were seen feeding in the morning, for if not disturbed they were sure to return toward the latter part of the day. And now for the hard work of goose shooting — digging the pits. Charlie, Eben and myself took the lower end of the field whilst the others went to the upper end, a mile or so from us. After an hour's digging three very respectable pits were finished, about twelve feet apart and covered with short stubble, and so disguised that we were confident the most wary old gander would not harbor a suspicion of danger. We had placed our Danz profile decoys around us in most bewitching positions, taken frequent pulls at our water bottles and discussed all points as to how we would do it, when the birds came. Charlie has a new 10-gauge Westly Richards hammerless, Eben a 10-gauge Scott, both heavy guns, and were shooting five drams of powder and 1¼ ounces No. 2 shot. I was the odd one. I was then, and am now, a 16-gauge crank. The year previous I had taken two guns with me, 10 and 16-gauge, W. & C. Scott & Sons, and after one trial of the small gun, had never fired the other again. So there I sat in the middle pit with my "pop-gun" as they called it, and no end of chaff did I have to take. All I could say was, "Wait and see." To tell the truth I thought they might clean me out as they were both crack shots, and by shooting 1¼ ounces shot as against my little ⅞ ounces, they certainly had the advantage in a flock at least.

While all this talking was going on I had my eyes peeled in the direction of the lake. At half past three we had said "Time they began to come," and then I caught sight of a long undulating line low down, way over towards the Alkali waters. "Down, boys! Quick! Here they come!" and then all was excitement in an instant. On they came, saw the decoys and made straight for us, honking, necks outstretched, with lazy wing. I can't say who fired first, but we do know that we all had arisen and fired when the birds were twenty yards too far. In the clear air the great fellows looked to be right on to us when, in fact, our first shots were at sixty to seventy yards; if we had only waited they would have come right over us, but what is the use of kicking? We would know better next time, and besides, four Canada geese lay dead on the hard ground before us, the result of six barrels; not so bad.

I was to take the middle birds, Eben those to the left and Charlie the right. Two had fallen from the center but both avowed they had fired at the old gander that was slightly ahead and leading the gang. So it was ever after; I could not keep one or the other from shooting at my center birds. At any rate, I claimed them, as they had no business to shoot at them.

Now that the ice was broken, in came flock after flock, and by the booming guns at the far end of the field, we knew our friends were having sport too. Oh, for another hour of such excitement! The sport lasted but an hour and then not a goose was to be seen. It was grand. But somehow or other I heard no more from my friends to the right and left as to the shooting qualities of the "pop-gun." Once in a while Charlie had remarked in excellent French, ". you got that fellow, Billy." I found that if I got on to them I killed my goose slick and clean, but if I was not very careful and trusted any to scatter, I got left and no goose. But the flight had ceased and we gathered up our dead and what a pile they made. We had four or five different kinds — pure white fellows with black on the ends of the wings; and one yellow legged fellow that the natives called a California goose, with a breast all blotched with black, looking as though he had been wounded the year before and black had grown instead of the original yellowish gray; great big Canada geese and smaller ones that seemed nearly the same.

Soon the two from the other ground came in with the wagon and our pile was counted and found to contain fifty-eight geese. Whoop la! Talk about fun, well that was a sample of it. Back to the little village in the soft twilight such as comes over the great Dakota prairies after a bright October day, with song and laughter and tale of how this one missed and that one hit, we came among the twinkling lights of the station. Soon Bob comes in from the slough and reports ducks without end but says he did not shoot well or would have had more game. We all say that same thing. However, his geese and great greenhead mallards added to our already shamefully large pile. All hands turned in and the birds were soon drawn, tied in bunches and expressed to friends in St. Paul and elsewhere. Then supper, smoke the pipe of peace while arranging for the next day's fray, and then sleep. In the morning two of our genial friends and companions took the train for Fargo there to join us Monday morning on our way home. How they hated to go and we equally regretted their departure, but business was to be attended to, so we bade them goodbye and promised a good report of our doings for the two days we were to stay.

After breakfast was eaten Mr. Long's express was brought to the door and in we piled, bound for the slough and mallards. Arriving at our destination we took possession of a small shanty used by some hardy pioneer as a roosting place when tilling the large fields around us. No other buildings were in sight. To the southward for two or three miles stretched the slough and such a place as it proved to be for water fowl.

To complete this story at this late date, February 16th, 1907, I can not help but comment upon the terrific change that has taken place since the events related took place.

The big slough just mentioned, in later years we came to know as Lake Etta Slough and the Big Slough back of Sam Devore's house. For years the latter slough has been dry. In 1884, it was almost a sea, although the bottom was hard and with rubber boots one could wade a good ways into it. Such clouds of water fowl as we saw here and at Sibley Lake and Buffalo Lake (all places that became familiar to us later on at Dawson) I have never seen before and never have seen since. I remember standing on the edge of the Sam Devore Slough when something alarmed the water fowl and they fairly darkened the sky when they got up, and the roar reminded one of a heavy train moving at a rapid rate of speed over a long, resonant trestle.

The first afternoon, E. waded in the smart-weed and the duck grass that hardly came to his knees and put up and killed 17 mallards. The team followed along opposite on the bank and as fast as he got two or three birds he put them in the wagon. He had been bragging a good deal about his shooting, a habit of conceit that has stuck to him all these years. So I made up my mind the next evening that I would take it out of him a bit. Bob and I had lugged our soap boxes out to an advantageous point for the evening flight, for we were satiated with shooting and had been loafing around all day. The soap boxes were an invention of Bob's as a seat, so we could squat down without breaking our legs or getting wet. I was shooting my 16-gauge gun and about the first bird that came along was a snow goose up quite high, but I covered it and let go a load of 6's and the bird folded up and fell within a few feet of where I was sitting, absolutely stone dead. Though dictating this more than twenty years after the event, the picture is as plain in my memory now as it was the day it happened.

At dusk, just as the great red glow of the gorgeous Dakota sunset was at its best in the west, the ducks began to come fast and furious. I do not think I shot more than twenty minutes. My gun was hot. Frequently I had to dodge to avoid being hit by the teal coming into the hole like bullets. Sometimes they came so fast and so low and close they startled me and I put up my arm to shield them off. It seemed as if they must knock me over. I only shot those that passed between me and the clear, red bit of sky and would fall free in the open water, for I never then nor do I now permit myself to shoot ducks that would fall in the rushes and can not be found. So with this brief shooting spell, fast and furious as it was, nearly all the birds fell in the open. I did not attempt to pick them up that night. The trail was long back to the hard ground, although the water was only knee deep.

E. had a pretty fair bag. He was rubbing it into the rest of us as usual. I said nothing but asked him to go out with me and help me pick up my birds in the morning. I remember I picked up and brought in 46 ducks besides the goose and they were largely teal and mallards. This was going some. It took the wind out of E.'s sails. It does not sound very well today; it is sort of game-hoggish. We had not at that time begun to appreciate that game was disappearing. The year before I had partaken of a buffalo hump in Montana and it was the last piece of wild buffalo meat I ever ate.

This ended our shooting. Two days with the ducks and one with the geese was sufficient. There were no laws in those days regarding shipment of game out of the state and we were able to bring home a fine lot of birds to our friends.

We commenced going to Dawson with the car, Saginaw, a year after this and continued to do so every year until 1899.

THE PORTABLE HOUSE, BUFFALO LAKE, SASK. (1912)

Left to right — W. B. Mershon, Jr., E. N. Briggs, Thos. Collins, G. D. Seib, Chas. M. Greenway, Bert Morley, Marden, the cook, W. B. Mershon and George Grant.

Western Trips

AFTER the goose shooting at Dawson, N. D., had played out we looked around for another location.

In 1900 we went to Pleasant Lake, north and west of Devil's Lake, N. D. In 1904 we erected a portable house at Buffalo Lake, about twenty-five miles north of Moose Jaw. We had shipped it by freight some time in advance, and it together with several boats, was awaiting our arrival. George Morley, Chase Osborn, later governor of the state of Michigan, and the writer went out and erected it. The wagon that carried it down the big hill had upset and we had a good hard job getting the house completed.

The plan was for part of the party to hunt geese a few days at Caron, a station just west of Moose Jaw. Then the three of us would go over to the lake, erect the house and the balance of the party would follow and finish our hunting with duck shooting.

C. H. Davis kept the log for that trip and I am copying it mainly for the purpose to show the comparison at the present time and years to come with the change that time has wrought. Goose shooting in the stubble fields around the Moose Jaw district has been a thing of the past for a number of years.

The old portable house served us well for ten years.

Assinaboia was consolidated with Saskatchewan. By the end of the ten years I had purchased a wheat ranch on the shores of Buffalo Lake, deeded same to my eldest son, and erected a bungalow on the lake shore where we have all the comforts of home. We no longer take the hunting car but we do go there each autumn for duck shooting which seems to be just as good as ever. Most of our shooting now is confined to canvasback and mallard.

Our party for the shooting trip of 1904 on the car, "W B. Mershon," left Saginaw the fourth of October and consisted of George Dan Seib of New York, E. N. Briggs then of San Francisco, W. A. Avery of Detroit, Chase S. Osborn of Sault Ste. Marie and the following from Saginaw: C. H. Davis, Watts S. Humphrey, Geo. B. Morley, Farnham Lyon and W. B. Mershon — nine, of whom today but three are living.

The forepart of the record I am omitting, and am starting with Friday, October 7th, the first day of our shooting. Davis's notes:

"Put out at 7.00 A. M. with four rigs for our first day's shoot. Mr. Stinson (schoolmaster) drove Mershon, Seib and Davis with the black team, ten and one-half miles west to the Sturgeon farm. Avery, Osborn, Morley and Humphrey stopped about two miles east of this in a big lighting—a great many geese and sandhill cranes in this vicinity. First party put in three pits and got out decoys at 11.00 A. M. Day overcast and brisk N. W. wind. First party left the pits at Sturgeon farm at 5.00 P. M. after killing 57 geese and 6 sandhill cranes (called turkeys about here). Major Lyon and Mr. Briggs hunted chickens in the forenoon and got five; Avery and Osborn 2 geese, Morley and Humphrey 7 geese.

Record for the day:

66 geese
6 sandhill cranes
5 chickens (sharp tailed grouse)
1 jackrabbit
—
78

SATURDAY, OCT. 8TH.

Cloudy and S. E. wind all day.

Two loads went after geese at the Sturgeon farm and thereabouts. Mershon, Seib and Davis, and Humphrey and Briggs drove to Pelican Lake. Saw many ducks, plover and curlew. This lake is really a big slough, about 18 miles long, little or no cover and disagreeable shooting. Mershon and Davis knocked down about a dozen ducks and one goose, recovering only 5 ducks. Mershon, Seib and Davis then drove over west among the hills for chicken. Saw about 40 but were very wild and got none.

Record for the day:

14 geese
1 sandhill crane
5 ducks
—
20

SUNDAY, OCT. 9TH.

Fine day. Messrs. Mershon, Morley and Osborn left the car at 8.00 A. M. with two rigs for Buffalo Lake to look after getting up portable house and report game prospects. Afternoon Seib and Davis prospected for geese north and west. Saw 1,800 to 2,000 geese.

MONDAY, OCT. 10TH.

Warm day, light S. W. wind.

Humphrey, Avery and Briggs pitted for geese on the Wilson place ten miles N. W. and got 23 geese and 1 crane. Seib, Lyon and Davis eight miles north on the Sheldon place — 80 rods west of schoolhouse — got 6 Canada geese. Receiving no word from our Buffalo Lake party as we expected, all made preparations for another day's hunt here tomorrow.

Record for the day:

29 geese
1 sandhill crane
—
30

TUESDAY, OCT. 11TH.

Fine day. Brisk S. and S. E. wind all day.

Humphrey, Briggs and Avery shot one-half mile south of Wilson place (ten miles N. W.) and got 7 geese. Seib, Lyon and Davis at Landervilles, sixteen miles N. W and six miles N. W of Wilson's, got 7 geese.

Record for the day — 14 geese.

Mershon sent out word by Wm. Beesley for party to come out to Buffalo Lake, or such as chose to do so.

WEDNESDAY, OCT. 12TH.

Seib, Avery and Davis left at 10.00 A. M. for Buffalo Lake with Beesley's rig and one rig from here, besides heavy team to take out the supplies and personal dunnage. Reached J. G. Beesley's at 11.45 where we took dinner and waited for the heavy team which arrived at 1.30 P. M. Left here at 2.00 P. M. arriving at Assinaboia Lodge on Buffalo Lake at 3.30 P. M. The following gentlemen remained on car at Caron — Humphrey, Lyon and Briggs with Alphonse, Charlie, the cook, going with the Buffalo Lake party. Distance from Caron to Beesley's, sixteen miles; to lodge on Buffalo Lake, twenty-six to twenty-seven miles. miles.

RECORD AT BUFFALO LAKE

Kept by W B. Mershon

SUNDAY, OCT. 9TH.

Mershon, Morley and Osborn arrived at the lake at 1.45 P. M. and began setting up the portable house and slept under the stars that night. Chas. L. C. Nabess and wife, on whose land the house was erected were very helpful, Mrs. Nabess baking bread and furnishing milk, etc. Weather warm, but cool at night.

MONDAY, OCT. 10TH.

Had a long, hard day's work and with Charlie's help completed the lodge, set up the stove with pipe furnished by the half breed, cooked supper and went to bed very, very tired. Weather fine.

TUESDAY, OCT. 11TH.

Shot a few ducks and geese before breakfast. Wm. Beesley left for Caron this A. M. to notify balance of party that everything was in readiness for all, or such of them, as might desire to come on to the lake, and bring in supplies, etc. Wind from the south and still blowing hard at bedtime. W. B. Mershon went two miles north in boat and got 38 ducks, mostly bluebills. Osborn shot at Green's Point, without boat, and killed 63 ducks, none of which he could bring in without a boat; got 2 grouse. Morley 7 ducks. The half breed killed 80 ducks today, about one-third mallards.

Record for the day: 45 ducks, 2 grouse — 47.

WEDNESDAY, OCT. 12TH.

Calm and cloudy. Osborn recovered 48 of the 63 ducks he killed yesterday and killed 8 more ducks today, also 5 grouse; Morley 2 ducks and Mershon 9.

Record for the day: 67 ducks, 5 grouse — 72.

Seib, Avery and Davis, with the cook and baggage wagon arrived late this afternoon.

THURSDAY, OCT. 13TH.

Calm, bright and warm.

Morley, who was paddled up to the head of the lake by Osborn shot away all his shells (150) by 3.00 P. M.

Balance of party had but little shooting until late in the day.

Record for the day: 62 ducks, 6 grouse, 4 yellowlegs — 72.

FRIDAY, OCT. 14TH.

Record for the day: 62 ducks.

SATURDAY, OCT. 15TH.

South wind, dark and misty. Cleared up bright and warm later in the day.

Davis, Seib and Mershon drove down to Green's Point, taking along the canvas boat. Shot there until noon and picked up 118 ducks out of a total of 137 knocked down, of which 126 were killed. After partaking of a hearty lunch of ham and eggs, etc., and after a good rest started back for the same place at 3.00 P. M. with Jesse and the sorrel team. When within half a mile of destination and driving slowly along a sideling piece of road, the left hand wheel suddenly collapsed without warning and pitched us all headlong. As sudden as it was and at the instant of our descent, Capt. Bill with his usual presence of mind yelled "Whoa!" to the horses and in the same breath inquired if anyone was hurt. The team stopped instantly and on picking ourselves up and inventorying the damage, were thankful to find no one hurt except Mr. Seib, who had a slight abrasion of the scalp from contact with one of the gun barrels. Giving Jesse instructions how to bind up his crippled wagon to get it back to the lodge, we walked on to the point and shot an hour or so getting 35 more ducks out of 45 knocked down, making a total for this party for the day of 182 ducks knocked down, of which 161 were killed and 153 recovered, notwithstanding Mr. Seib who suffered with a severe headache, did no shooting after 11.00 A. M. Balance of party got 54 ducks, 2 geese and 3 grouse.

Record for the day: 2 geese, 207 ducks, 3 grouse — 212.

SUNDAY, OCT. 16TH.

Closed up the house and left beautiful Buffalo Lake at 10.30 A. M. Drove to Beesley's (11 miles) for dinner and arrived at Caron (15 miles farther) at 4.40 P. M. Found car party all well and Mr. Humphrey furnishes the following as the record of game killed by himself, Lyon and Briggs for the 12th, 13th, 14th and 15th as follows: 4 geese, 1 crane, 18 grouse — 23.

MONDAY, OCT. 17TH.

All hands went out this morning for a goose shoot (except Lyon and Briggs). Mershon, Morley and Osborn, also Seib and Davis left at 8.00 A. M. and drove 16 miles to Landervilles and found that the geese had mostly left this vicinity, so turned about and all drove east, parting at Wilson's place. Seib and Davis put in two pits on the widow Flax's place two miles south of Harry Brown's (Government Reservoir). Got into pits at 2.30 P. M. and got 8 geese. Mershon party got 7. Humphrey and Avery with Willie Beesley 13, Lyon and Briggs 1 grouse.

Record for the day: 28 geese, 1 grouse — 29.

TUESDAY, OCT. 18TH.

All but Lyon and Briggs got up at 3.30 A. M. for an early shoot. Started out at 4.45. Seib and Davis shot the pits at widow Flax's farm in the morning. Clear with light S. W. wind. Geese came out too high. Knocked down but one goose which could not be found. Then drove three miles to Pelican Lake and saw the flight come in very high. Went back to Harry Brown's field and took natural cover at noon. Geese came out late, between 4.00 and 5.00 P M. Killed 9 geese and picked up one of yesterday's shoot, 10 in all. Mershon party got 11; Humphrey and Avery 11; Lyon and Briggs 14 grouse.

Record for the day: 32 geese, 14 grouse, 2 jack-rabbits — 46.

The weather being mild and clear the geese kept very high both coming and going to and from their food and would not decoy well and the flights were becoming more scattered.

Hon. Chase S. Osborn made the record for long distance shooting today, killing five long shots while lying down in the road from flights going over.

After all were assembled at the car about 7.30 P M. it was voted that we pull out for home, thus ending a most delightful outing and shoot."

The big day's duck shooting of October 15th took place on a very cloudy day. The ducks were almost entirely bluebills. It was very sporty shooting, and I was shooting better that day than I ever did before or since, for it seemed as if I could hit every duck I shot at. Of the total of 182 ducks, 161 of them were killed stone dead and but 21 crippled. Considering the severity of the wind the percentage we were able to pick up was very good indeed.

Our surplus birds were given at that time to the half breed, who was a market hunter, and we arranged with him if he would not hunt during the time we were there but would help us with his team and services and take the ducks to town we would give them to him. If he had been shooting at that time for the market he probably would have killed more birds than we did, and he was well satisfied with the bargain and it relieved us of the worry of what was to become of our birds.

GREAT WHOOPING CRANE

Now nearly extinct. When we hunted around Dawson, N. D., between 1884 and 1890 we saw these birds almost daily. They fed in the wheat fields the same as the Sandhill Crane. The bird from which this picture was taken was killed at Buffalo Lake, north and east of Moose Jaw, Sask., in 1904, and stands as mounted, four feet, four inches in height.

The Dance of the Sandhill Crane

ONE of the strangest freaks of nature is the crane dance, so-called, — the dance of the sandhill crane.

Most birds that go through these grotesque maneuvers do so at the mating time, a nuptial dance, wherein the male endeavors to prove attractive to the female, like the dance of the prairie chicken or pinnated grouse, the strutting of the wild turkey and the song flight of the woodcock, or Wilson's snipe; but with the sandhill crane it was not so, for the dance which I am about to describe took place in October.

We had two large cranes in the northwest in the early days — the great whooping crane, a big white fellow nearly as tall as a man, and now unfortunately nearly as extinct as the passenger pigeon; the other was the sandhill crane, which must not be confounded with our blue heron, the frog eater of the marshes, for the sandhill crane is an upland bird, not as plentiful now as it was thirty years ago.

It was about 1889 that I was goose shooting in Kidder County, North Dakota. It was about the 10th of October. I had driven north from Dawson the day before — about fifteen miles — for I had learned that the geese were feeding on the stubble fields in that locality in quantity. My companion and I got to the feeding ground in time the night before to dig our goose pits and get them stubbled, so that they were well disguised, and we slept that night on a very cold, hard floor. I know, because they were digging a cellar underneath this farmer's shack and the wind came up through the cracks so that it was a most uncomfortable night and long before daylight we were glad to get up, and after a hurried bite get away to the pits in the stubble field.

We were side by side, our pits not more than a dozen feet apart, the decoys out, and comfortably settled as the sky was reddening in the east, toward which we were facing. We were on the lower side of a slight hill whose crest was outlined against the reddening sky. Before the sun had shown its rim above the horizon, we saw coming from various directions, sandhill cranes in twos and threes and in flocks of fifteen or twenty. They came from every direction, silent and without a call, centering on the hill crest some three or four hundred yards in front of us and directly toward the sunrise.

Silently they alighted and formed a great circle. All didn't join in the circle at once; a few seemed to stand aloof as audience or onlookers, but as the excitement increased, they too joined the dancing throng. These birds, all facing inward and silhouetted against the sky, made a most grotesque picture. They did not dance in unison; first one would drop a wing, another would raise a wing, they would stand on one foot and then another, their great long necks and heads would bow to the ground and then be raised on high, but they were all busily hopping, bowing and scraping and flapping their wings at the same time. They didn't go around in a circle but maintained much the same position.

They kept their weird and strange performance up for about eight or ten minutes. By that time the sun had shown itself above the sky line and at a signal, that we did not hear, the dancing ceased as quickly as it had begun, and one by one or in groups of a dozen or more, these cranes left as silently as they had come, flying in all directions. Some came over us, so we took toll out of them. They were goodly birds, with a body like a young turkey and when roasted were just as good, in fact, we preferred them to any of the other game unless it was the sharptailed grouse, but the roasted crane we always thought was the choice morsel compared to young wild goose, duck or even the canvasback.

Trout Fishing in Michigan

MY FIRST trout fishing took place when I was about eighteen years old. My father was shipping lumber to Saginaw from near Clare on the Pere Marquette Railway.

West of Clare a few miles on the Tobacco River was Hinkle's dam. I believe the Wilsons of Farwell drew lumber there for shipping, but whether there was a mill originally at this dam, I don't know, and I haven't taken the pains to find out, but at any rate, a big pool had been formed below the dam, as is always the case. This may have been a dam for flooding the stream to run the saw logs, for Michigan streams in the early days had many of these dams.

My father had discovered that in the big pool below the dam there were some very fine brook trout. He brought a half dozen ten or twelve-inch fellows back with him from a previous trip, and I recall he had them done up in a handkerchief. So when he went back the following week I was asked to go along, and there I caught my first Michigan brook trout.

I had taken a trout before in Canada, for when the boats were running in the good old days it was quite the custom for my father and a number of our neighbors to take the whole family and go over to Goderich, Ont., and spend a few weeks in the summer, and I had accompanied the party to Ben Miller's mill of Ben

MICHIGAN GRAYLING

Taken from Black River in 1903

Millersville, and had there with a worm taken my first trout.

I, of course, fished with bait; hadn't learned to fly fish when I made this first trip to the Tobacco River, and as I recall it, the driftwood and rejected lumber that nearly covered the surface of the pool would have prevented fly fishing anyhow, but between the cracks and crevices a big juicy worm was lowered and I was rewarded with several nice trout. These were the result of the planting made by my father and some other Saginaw gentlemen in 1870.

Brook trout were not native to the Lower Peninsula of Michigan and all were man planted to begin with, with the exception of those that were found in the streams that fringed the extreme upper part of the Lower Peninsula. These fish undoubtedly came from Lake Superior. The grayling and the brook trout existed together in the Jordan for sometime. All streams that are now trout streams in the Lower Peninsula, or nearly all of them, were originally grayling streams.

As I said before, in 1870 the first trout were planted by A. H. Mershon, my father. The fry was obtained from Seth Green of Caledonia, N. Y. In running down this early history of the brook trout in Michigan I had occasion to write to George M. Brown, who was in the engineering department of the F. & P. M. Railroad for many years, and was at one time one of the Fish Commissoners in Michigan. His letter written from West Palm Beach, Fla., Feb. 7th, 1920, follows:

My Dear Sir:

The most reliable information that I have is that brook trout were native to all streams from the Jordan River on the west to Rogers City on the east. South of that to the Saginaw Bay on the east and Muskegon on the west, the grayling were plentiful. South of that we find bass, perch, pike and numerous other fish.

The end of the Flint and Pere Marquette Railroad in 1868 was at Averill; in 1869 and early '70, it was completed to the lake. Mr. A. H. Mershon and others of Saginaw secured some brook trout fry from Seth Green at Caledonia, N. Y., and planted them in the spring of 1870 in brooks tributary to the South Branch of the Tobacco River west of Clare and about Farwell.

In 1871 I assisted the first State Fish Commissioner to catch grayling at or near Reed City from which to get eggs for propagation. After the state fish hatchery was built at Paris and the U. S. operated or had taken over the Clark Hatchery at Northville, we began to get brook trout fry for the streams tributary to the Pere Marquette. In 1874 the superintendent, Mr. Sanford Keeler, built a business car which, as Superintendent of Roadway and Structures, I used a great deal, and as the Railroad Company and many of our sportsmen friends received notice of an assignment of trout fry, they were turned over to me to distribute with this car because we could stop anywhere, at all the small brooks tributary to the streams in Clare, Osceola, Lake and Mason Counties. After 1883 we reached the Sauble, Little Manistee and Manistee Rivers, also the North Branch of the Tobacco River and the Cedar River east of Harrison.

As to the date we first received any rainbow, known then as California trout, I do not remember. The record of the hatcheries may show, but I do know that we took pains to plant them in the larger streams, like the Muskegon, the Marquette, the Sauble and the Manistee because they grow rapidly, want big water and will thrive in water that is ten degrees warmer than brook trout will stay in.

I never tried to get any German Brown Trout, "Lock Levan." They are such cannibals that I do not think they should have any place in our streams. You might as well plant grass pike there. Nor are German carp wanted in our St. Clair River and Saginaw Bay waters.

If you can pick out anything of use to you in this, I will be glad.

Very truly yours,

GEO. M. BROWN.

The business car Mr. Brown alludes to was named the "Peggy" and I am fortunate in having a photograph of it to reproduce herewith. It was christened "The Peckanese," but was soon nicknamed "The Peggy." I will have more to tell of the "Peggy" later on.

Mr. Sanford Keeler, who was Superintendent of the F. & P. M. Railway from the time of its origin until not many years ago, has allowed me to copy a letter that he wrote at my request December 1919:

DEAR SIR:

I have a letter from Mr. W. B. Mershon of this place asking me to inform you regarding nativity of brook trout in Michigan. I do not know of any stream in Michigan where they existed before planting unless it may have been the Jordan River, which I doubt of its being their home originally, as brook trout and grayling do not prosper long together. The trout are too voracious for them.

The first time that I knew of any trout being planted was by Mr. A. H. Mershon, the father of Wm. B. Mershon, about the year 1869 or '70, in the Tobacco River about three miles west of Clare. Some four years later I arranged with F. W. Clark, then of Northville, for a supply of the fry from the Northville Hatchery, which with Mr. Geo. M. Brown, whom I was associated with as an official on the F & P. M. Railway, we stocked or planted several thousands in the streams that the railroad crossed — Twin Creek at Evart, Hersey River between Hersey and Reed City, Sanborn Creek west of Nirvana, Marquette River near Baldwin, Kinne Creek west of Baldwin, and some small streams on the Harrison Branch. This planting and restocking continued for several years, and results were satisfactory.

My memory is not very clear as to date, but what I have given is practically correct. I received several cans of fry from Big Rapids on the G. R. & I. Railroad after the Northville Hatchery was abandoned.

Your truly,

SANFORD KEELER.

A most interesting article written by Walter J. Hunsaker, at that time President of the Michigan Fish Commission, I am also privileged to reproduce:

Saginaw, December 1919.

Why brook trout (Savelinus Fontinalis) were not native to the whole of the upper half of the Lower Peninsula has always been a subject of fascinating speculation to those who have taken interest in the history of that fish in Michigan.

So far back as has been traced brook trout existed indigenously to some extent in the streams that emptied into the vicinity of the Straits of Mackinac from the Lower Peninsula, but there were none in streams south of that locality; all the latter, clear, cold, spring-fed brooks and rivers, were the home of the grayling—the Micigan grayling, a distinct specie. Except for the coast region from Traverse City on the Lake Michigan side to Rogers City on the Lake Huron side, practically all the brook trout that have inhabited the Lower Peninsula waters were artificially bred and artificially planted.

The records show, as reliably as could be expected in regard to a subject of this character, that Upper Peninsula streams contained brook trout when the white man first adventured into its wilds. There is a belief that the Upper Peninsula trout worked across Lake Superior from the Nepigon River country, and thence in the course of time across the Straits into the upper fringe of the Lower Peninsula. Perhaps — but if so, it was so long ago that there is no authentic data upon the hegira.

Where the grayling once had an exclusive established home in the Southern Peninsula, he is known no more in all his silver rainbow beauty. Salvelinus Fontinalis occupies his place in as great, if not greater, abundance. Artificial planting in those former grayling waters, through the overturning of Nature's plan by man, has been an unqualified success, so far as brook trout is concerned. It is then of interest to ascertain the first plantings of brook trout in this state.

There is no difficulty in finding the first official planting so to speak—that is, by the state, for the records of the Michigan Fish Commission show that. The Commission was organized under the act of April 19, 1873. But it was not until 1879—five years after organization, that the Commission artificially hatched from wild eggs and planted brook trout. In the first report of the first Commission, signed by George Clark, A. J. Kellogg and Gov. John J. Bagley (1873-74) it appears that the principal fishes in which the state was concerned were white fish and lake trout; only brief mention of the brook trout is made, a small paragraph, while two pages and a half are devoted to the history and habits of the Atlantic salmon and other pages to the land-locked salmon, the "California salmon," the shad and the eel.

But of course the Commission was merely groping then—it had not wholly found itself and the scope of its true work. It is not until the fourth report (1880), that any further mention is made of brook trout—nothing at all in the second and third reports. But in the fourth report the Fish Commission begins to regard the brook trout as of some importance, and it calls him "Salmo Fontinalis." It says:

> "We have become satisfied that this fish (brook trout) is capable of a much wider range throughout the state than was formerly supposed. Some having escaped from private ponds into the different streams in almost all parts of the state, have so grown and multiplied as to leave no doubt of the perfect practicability of their successful introduction and propagation in nearly all of the smaller streams."

So they ventured upon experimental hatching at the Pokagon Hatchery, with pretty bad luck. Out of about 470,000 eggs which they put on the trays at Pokagon during two seasons, only a very small percentage hatched or lived to be planted—about 60,000. This was in 1878-79. On February 16th, 1880, in the Townships of Shelby, Hart and Eldridge in Oceana County, in Fly, Spring, Ludd & Hand's, Russell's,

Doolett's, Damorell's, Tennant's, Hiles', Andrus' and Generaw Creeks—the Commission's first planting was made—4,500 brook trout fry. To E. D. Richmond of Hart is to be accorded the distinction of personally planting the state's first successful hatching of brook trout. In all 50,400 fry of this first Pokagon hatching was planted that year—1880—in Allegan, Berrien, Cass, Calhoun, Clare, Kalamazoo, Kent, Mecosta, Newaygo, Oceana, Osceola, Van Buren, Washtenaw and Wexford Counties.

From this date the hatching and planting went on progressively. There were 251,000 fry planted in 1882, something over 500,000 in 1883-4 and in 1885 and 1886 for the first time the total planting for two years went slightly over the million mark. Now the present Michigan Fish Commission plants about 25,000,000 every two years. For the coming year alone, the plant will probably be close to 15,000,000.

But who was the first person to *privately* hatch and plant brook trout fry in the state? It is evident from the foregoing extract from the fourth report of the Fish Commission in 1880 that the Commission was moved to take up the work of state propagation by the fact that fish that "had escaped from private ponds," had grown and multiplied in different streams of the state; so it is certain that a good deal of amateur propagation of brook trout had been under way for a considerable time.

I can add but little to the meagre fund of information on this most interesting point, but probably

N. W. Clark of Clarkston was among the first. It is of record that in 1867 Mr. Clark had private ponds at Clarkston in which he raised stock fish and hatched fry from their eggs with considerable success. It is said that he began these experiments a "year or two after the war," so that at least his work was under way in 1866. Whether he distributed his fry into public waters there is no record, but he was a most public spirited man, intensely interested in fish life, was one of the main forces behind the movement to establish a state department of fish culture and gave much of his time and private means to this end. Therefore, it is wholly probable that he planted the product of his little Clarkston hatchery in convenient streams for the benefit of the general public. This view is borne out too, by the fact that Mr. Clark with Daniel Fitzhugh of Bay City made a small planting of rainbow trout in the Au Sable in the middle seventies, although the late Frank N. Clark, Superintendent of the government hatchery at Northville, said in 1909 that these fry came from fish that had been placed in the ponds at Northville before 1876, but he could not remember where the parent fish came from.

So far as any authentic records show, this was the first planting of rainbow trout in Michigan. It was not until 1880 that the Fish Commission made a planting of rainbows. In that year the Commission raised 1,800 fry from eggs contributed by the U. S. Commission of Fisheries. 600 were planted in the Paw Paw River in Van Buren County and 600 in Boyne River,

Charlevoix County, and the rest were kept at the hatchery for stock fish.

In that year, incidentally, we get the first intimation of the coming of that destructive fish hog—the German Carp. The Commissioners report records that "Prof. Baird (U. S. Commissioner) on the 5th of November last sent 20 pairs of this fish to the state" and the Commission promises "to do all in its power to increase their distribution throughout the state," because "they must be admirably adapted to our warm shallow lakes." It was not until 1889, however, that the first planting of fry was made, when 20,000 carp were distributed.

Here arrives also the year of the German Brown trout (it seemed to be a pretty good year for Germans); for the Commission put into the state's waters in 1889 its first hatching of browns—20,000 fry which went into the inlet of Deer Lake at Boyne Falls. Whether there was ever any private planting of German Brown prior to 1889, I do not know.

WALTER J. HUNSAKER.

Additional evidence on the early history of the "Speckled" trout comes in a letter dated Dec. 21st, 1921, from Seymour Bower, Supt. of Fisheries for Michigan for many years. This letter is in reply to my inquiry and follows:

MY DEAR MR. MERSHON:

As to the southern limit of native trout streams in Michigan, I think it is very well established that native trout had worked down as far south as the Boardman and its tributaries, but no farther; and that they inhabited most if not all of the streams flowing into Lake Michigan between the Boardman and the Straits. This was the conclusion arrived at by John H. Bissell of Detroit, a member of the Fish Commission, who made some investigations along this line many years ago. Confirming this conclusion in part, is the evidence of a few old timers at Charlevoix whom I questioned on this subject twenty-six or twenty-seven years ago this winter, while I was stationed at Charlevoix a few weeks installing a 200 jar whitefish battery as a branch of the Detroit house. These old settlers stated in the most positive way that brook trout inhabited all the streams thereabout long before young trout were sent to that section for planting.

Regarding the Lake Huron streams south of the Straits, I think Bissell is not so certain as to how far down the trout had worked, but believe he concluded that Hammond's Bay or not far below was the dividing line. Mr. Bissell's address is Bank Chambers Building, Detroit, and I suggest that you correspond with him.

As to the first planting of trout in Michigan, I confess I do not know, but there is no doubt that the first efforts in the way of *hatching* and *raising* brook trout in this state were made by N. W. Clark, of Clarkston, Oakland County. This was during the first season, or possibly the second, following the close of the Civil War; that is, the trout hatching season of '66-'67 or

'67-'68. His trout plant was small and in the rough as compared to a layout like that at Paris today. It was located near Clarkston depot, about two miles southwest of Clarkston village. The water supply was quite limited, drawn from one or more small spring creeks. The first trout I ever saw were in his ponds at that point; though I had often heard my father, who came from "York State," tell about catching brook trout from brooks near his home in Tompkins County.

Clark also built a small hatchery in Clarkston village, in a gorge or valley below the millpond, mainly for hatching whitefish and salmon, the water being a gravity flow from the pond above. A small supply of spring water near this hatchery also enabled him to carry a small pool or two of brook trout, mainly I suppose for experimental and exhibition purposes. Clark had no previous experience in fish culture but gained what information he could by personal interview with Seth Green and an inspection of Green's layout. Green also supplied Clark with his first trout eggs and "coached" him in the business, which proved successful as a fish culture enterprise on what would now be considered a small scale, but it was not a money maker. However, it was sufficiently promising financially to induce Clark to seek another location affording a greater supply of spring water, so in 1873 he pulled up stakes and transferred his activities to Northville, where at that time there was an available supply or flow of spring water amounting to 300 to 400 gallons per minute.

Now, either from his own production or purchase of

eggs elsewhere, Clark must have had something of a surplus of trout fry or fingerlings for sale or planting, from the Clarkston work, prior to 1870, but if so I have no definite information as to what became of them; and it is doubtful as to whether the facts covering this part of his early work can be dug up. I am now living within five miles of Clarkston and during the winter will endeavor to interview a few old timers there that are still hanging on; also expect to call at Northville this winter and may find something on this point in the U. S. hatchery reports.

Hoping I have not overtaxed your patience with this lengthy and rambling account drawn from memory, and wishing you a very enjoyable holiday season and many of them I remain,

Very sincerely yours,
SEYMOUR BOWER.

It wasn't many years after the trout were known to be in the streams around Farwell and Clare that a number of my companions began to develop as anglers, and the first trout fishing that I did after the excursion to Clare was with Jack and George Morley, Thomas Harvey, Eben Briggs and two or three other chums of mine. My father died in 1884 and for a year or two previous to his death had been unable to go afield.

By the damming of the Tobacco River at Farwell, a considerable pond or lake was created and we discovered that there were trout in this pond, or especially at the head of it where the little stream came into it, and also just below the dam where the pond discharged.

We used to get from Sanford Keeler, the genial Superintendent of the Pere Marquette Railroad, his business car, "The Peggy," and all of us being hard at work six days of the week, there was only Sunday reserved for our fishing trips. With Frank Hatswell to drive the engine, we would get aboard it at Saginaw before daylight. Jack Morley, always a tinkerer and an inventor, had what was then a novelty—a kerosene heater or stove that was very smoky and smelly, but with it after we were under way, he would make a great big pot of strong coffee. We had an ample supply of lunch in baskets and boxes, so that our Sunday morning breakfast was just at the crack of day as the Peggy was speeding west towards Farwell. We had a clear track, for there was no Sunday traffic. A side track ran down to the little flouring mill that stood at the dam on Farwell Lake, so the Peggy would be run in there, and we were on hand for quite early Sunday morning fishing.

Our catches never were large, but they were satisfactory. We were worm fishermen in those days; hadn't mastered the art of fly fishing, but we had a glorious time of it in those early May days. Perchance the arbutus was still in bloom, the phœbes nesting under the ledges of the old buildings, and blackbirds, bluebirds, white breasted swallows and all other birds were then at their best and everywhere.

Tired but happy we would be home shortly after

THE "PEGGY"

Private conveyance of Supt. Sanford Keeler of the Flint & Pere Marquette Railroad. Built in 1874. Cylinders 10 × 14; driving wheels 52" length of frame 33 ft., weight with fuel 40,000 lbs. It was wrecked in March 1893 carrying Geo. M. Brown on an inspection trip on the Lake Branch. It was then ordered dismantled by W. H. Baldwin, General Manager.

dusk. Jack Morley generally fell in and got a ducking. I don't recall ever going on a fishing trip with Jack that he didn't fall in.

After that we began going farther with the Peggy. Grayling were still very plentiful on the Little Manistee. W. D. Wing & Bro. were operating a lumber plant at Wingleton, four miles west of Baldwin in Lake County. The logs were brought in by a logging road, one end of which was not far from the Little Manistee River. We would go up on the regular train, sometimes with the Peggy. If we had the Peggy it was generally for a day's trip only to Kinne Creek, where by that time trout were plentiful, but the Creek had never been cleaned out and it was a mass of tangle and very hard to fish. Old Poquette, one of the sawmill men, regularly came in with a basket of large brook trout. He never would tell exactly where he got them or how he got them. He must have been a natural born kingfisher. We afterwards found that in the Austin Pond that headed up well on Kinne Creek and where we never had been to fish, the Frenchman got the big ones. The grayling fishing was superb in the old days.

W F. Dermont was then General Manager for Wing, a whole-souled, genial gentleman with whom I was in later years associated for nearly twenty years, he being the General Manager of a lumber company of which I was President that operated for that length of time at Williams, Arizona. On our arrival Dermont would have everything ready and we would get aboard the logging train that was fetching the logs into Mill Lake. On its return trip we would be loaded on one of the cars with our camping paraphernalia. How many miles we went I do not know, but we were dumped at the end of the road two or three miles from the Little Manistee River at the point called the "Snagging Shanties." A camp team would take us to that part of the River where we were to begin our fishing and then go down farther, generally to Dam 2 I think it was, where the tent would be put up and the camp established and whoever was to do the cooking for us left in charge. The team would go back to its work with instructions to call for us the next day or the day following or whatever it might be.

There were no trout in the Little Manistee in those days, and we waded the stream catching grayling. Some of them were enormous for grayling. Towards the last they were all big ones from 1½ to 1⅞ lbs. I think I have caught as large a Michigan Grayling as anyone ever caught, and by actual weight I never had one that would go 2 lbs., but I have had them frequently from 1½ to 1⅞ lbs.

It was here we introduced the art of fishing with the "Little Tin Boat," so called. It was a metal boat with a wooden bottom made by Bond of Cleveland, easily taken apart in the middle so it could be carried in the back end of a democrat wagon. It was locked together with two dovetails in the bottom and a pin driven through two eyes at the top of the gunnel, and tightened with a wedge shaped key, made a staunch, serviceable little boat. The middle seat was an air tight compartment. Two of us would start ahead with this boat until we had gone around four or five bends; then we would pull the boat on a sand bar or fasten it against the shore safely and go ahead with our fishing. The two behind us would fish until they came to the boat, then they would get in and run by us four or five bends, and this operation was repeated throughout the length of the day. It enabled us to fish a lot of stream, greatly lessened the fatigue and made a very practical vehicle for carrying our surplus luggage, lunch, etc. Then again we had a basket with an ice compartment that our fish after cleaning could be nicely laid away in for safe carrying in this boat. I say "safe carrying" reservedly, for there was hardly a trip that that boat didn't meet with a mishap. Either Jack Morley would get hung up on a cedar sweeper that he hadn't ducked low enough in running the boat under, or someone would go around one of the sharp bends where the current was extra swift and be swept to the outer side of the circle and tipped over, or something was pretty sure to happen, but nothing serious ever occurred.

What fishing we had! Grayling in quantity that now would be shocking. We would bring out on the logging train in the morning great chunks of ice. These were buried in the sand at the camping place and the fish at night were packed in a cool receptacle, so that they were kept in good condition. Once I remember when we returned from one of these trips, three or four of us having been out three days, we had a wash tub full of grayling. There was wonderful fishing at this dam too. A great pool below it was literally alive with large grayling, but the taking of these big fellows from the comparatively still pool did not begin with the sport of wading the rapid stream and taking one here and there. If I had known how to scientifically fish with a fly in those days, I am sure that I would have had more sport, but ignorance is bliss and I didn't know any better, or none of us did for that matter, than worm fishing.

Once a bear swam across the stream right near us. Another time we ran on to a heron rookery; there were hundreds and hundreds of blue herons perched or nesting in the tops of the pine and spruce forest. Deer we frequently saw. Once Jack Morley picked up a stone and threw it at a blue heron standing in the river fishing. He hit it in the neck and killed it, and tender heartedly regretted it the balance of the day. Sometimes there would be a forest fire. We would smell the smoke or see it and it would seem to be way off to one side of our course and suddenly the stream would make a sharp turn, and before we knew it we were right in the midst of the fire. Then it was duck ourselves in the water, hustle the boat by and get out of it the best we could, which we always did safely.

By and by we got a trout or two. Then the next year when we went up there we found the trout more plentiful and the grayling less. We began fishing up farther; got in at the county line or above it, fishing through the "Jungle," a place in the stream so filled with down timber that we had to get out and go around it and get in below. Those were indeed good old days.

Once I remember my brother Ned went with me. He never had fished before, a patient, quiet, artistic man. He became quite interested in the fishing before the day was done and beat us all at it, but he never went the second time, although he admitted that he had never had a better time in his life than he did the two or three days that he camped with me on the Little Manistee. Poor Ned, he died before his time—four years younger than I. Maybe had he loved the hunting and fishing, he would be here now.

It was not long before the grayling were all gone and we had very good brook trout fishing in the Little Manistee and its nearby neighbor—the Sauble, whose head waters were hard to get at. I didn't go there long, for other places were more attractive. Some of the boys fished Baldwin Creek; that was a great grayling stream in its day. Danaher Creek, a tributary putting into the Pere Marquette from the South, was early a wonderful trout stream. A chimney sweep here in Saginaw,—I knew him by no other name than "the chimney sweep"— used to bring down great baskets of trout from Danaher Creek and sell them. It was a little bit of a stream full of logs and rubbish. With a little short pole and bait, he patiently crawled on hands and knees to the favorite spots and literally yanked them out, but he was a good old sport just the same. He had to sell them or he couldn't have gone trout fishing.

After the grayling were nearly all gone, the only remaining ones being in the Black River, we began fishing on the North Branch of the Au Sable, the most wonderful trout stream in the world in its day, and it would be yet if it were not fished to death. It has been advertised and commercialized until at the present time during the trout season one can not make a cast without hooking someone on his back cast. They fish with spinners, trolling hooks, worms and minnows, as well as flies, and it just can not stand it any more, but when I first knew it, it was a wonder. There were no roads that we knew of up and down the river to any great extent, but there were the paths and trails made by the river drivers that always led along the river. Tom Judge had a sawmill at what is now Lovells. It was known as Judge's in those days. The Michigan Central had just built a branch in from Grayling to Twin Lakes or Lewiston. We could get a team and driver and a big lumber wagon of Judge and camp down stream and have him come after us at a certain day, or as we more often did, go in with our old private car, the "City of Saginaw," and side track it at Judge's mill. Waldo Avery was an old time fishing companion of mine, long since gone to his reward. Hardly a twist or a bend on that river, and many other rivers, have I visited in late years that I have not thought of my old friend Waldo and pictured some incident that occurred at that spot. For instance, on the very first trip that I ever made down the North Branch of the Au Sable as far as where the Morley and Kuehl cottages now stand, Waldo was my companion. A spring came out from the high bank sufficient to throw a jet of water several feet from the bank, then falling into the river. At the edge of this high bank was a deep pool, for all the high banks occur at a bend. Waldo and I had separated. He had gone down a little farther and was to come back and pick me up at quitting time. I had started above and that was to be my getting out place, where this stream spouted from the bank. I had a fine catch of brook trout. There wasn't a rainbow or anything else in there; it was before the days of the cannibal of all cannibals—the German brown trout. When Avery appeared on the bank and hollered to me I had just landed a 16-in. brook trout, and at the cast before that had put into my creel one 14-in. in length. Think of that now, ye anglers of the North Branch. What would you give for two such fish in one afternoon, or in one season, for that matter.

By the time we had begun to fish the North Branch of the Au Sable we had become adepts in fly fishing; in fact, before we left Kinne Creek we had learned to fly fish. There was no limit as to the number one might take, the only limit being how many one could carry or wanted. The state law said that anything under 6 in. must be put back, but on the North Branch we rarely got anything under 8 in. Later on an 8 in. law was put into effect, and fly fishing only allowed on that stream. A splendid law, and it should have been maintained, for while it was in operation the trout increased tremendously. Native trout had a chance to spawn and reproduce and we were not dependent entirely upon hatcheries for stocking the stream, but our legislators couldn't let well enough alone, and after a few years of practical demonstration of trout streams regulated in this way, they repealed the law, and it is as I stated a while back, no longer worth fishing.

Then we moved over to the Black River, a wonderful trout stream with miles of fishing water, and there were still a few grayling in the Black at late as 1903.

Many of the old companions of my fishing days have gone forever. Dear old Farnham Lyon—an old man when he first began going with us young fellows; one of the most kindly, lovable characters I ever knew; an excellent angler and a splendid partridge shot; always whistled when he filled a hand at poker, never used a cuss word and always looked as neat as if he just stepped out of a bandbox.

Inasmuch as the grayling are gone, rainbow trout now predominate in the North Branch of the Au Sable, and the brown trout are increasing, soon to drive out the remaining brook trout. I use these quotations from an old record to show when the grayling disappeared and how free the North Branch of the Au Sable was from all other fish than the brook trout, after the grayling. For a long time no rainbows were taken above Dam 4.

"June 20th, 1899. On the Main Au Sable River with Geo. Alexander, Watts S. Humphrey, Rube

Babbitt and guides. Camped at the mouth of the South Branch and fished three days. Weather unfavorable but I caught about 60 fish, a dozen of them being from 1 lb. to 1¾ lbs., mainly rainbows. I caught one grayling on the South Branch. I used a Floating Mayfly, cork body.
(Probably one of my first experiments with the dry fly.)

"On May 12th, 1900, we went to Lovells with a car party—ten of us. On May 14th I fished below and had 41 trout, all big ones; very hot. The party got 1,038 trout during this trip—the greatest fishing trip we ever had in Michigan. This is for ten men for three days, or an average of about 30 trout per day per man. We took only four rainbow trout, one a two pounder. These were taken about three miles below Dam 4.

"June 14th, 1901. Fishing the North Branch. We camped near Big Creek at "Father's Barn." That is where Paul Morley's house now stands, and was called "Father's Barn" because on a previous trip Tom Harvey was very uncomfortable (it was stormy and rainy) and Tom told of the homesick boy who said "I wish I was at father's barn," and on being asked "Why?" said, "Then I would be near enough to go into the house." On this trip the record speaks of rainbows seeming to be quite plentiful below Big Creek and that Waldo Avery took one 23 inches long that weighed 4¼ lbs. on a No. 8 Cahill. This was at the Blondy Dam on Big Creek."

"May 9th, 1902. Morley got two nice rainbow trout above where Big Creek comes into the North Branch. These were the only ones taken on this trip. We were taking 25 to 30 trout apiece a day with an 8 inch limit. On the 10th it snowed all morning, but Morley and I took 49 fish in the snowstorm. There were eight in the party for the four days fishing; took 400 fish, all with the fly."

In 1903 we had a camping trip on the Black River. We fished from the 29th of May to and including June 3rd, although two of the party came home two days before the others. The record says "a cold northeast wind all the time." There were seven in the party. Total catch was 346 brook trout and 46 grayling. The largest trout was 16 inches long, and the largest grayling 14½ inches long.

We were on the Black River on August 19th, 1903. Camped at Camp King. Water was very high and dirty from rains. Fished from McKinnon's Bend to the foot of the tag alders and I had 24 trout and one grayling. On the 20th the fishing was exceptionally fine. I took a grayling on that day and another on the 21st. The trout ran from 9 inches to 14 inches in length. The total catch for the three of us up to and including August 22nd was 398 brook trout and 11 grayling.

The record says, "I think 1903 was the last year of the grayling in the Lower Peninsula of Michigan."

The Michigan Grayling

(Thymalus Tricolor Cope)

ONE of our great writers has said, "Doubtless God could make a better berry than the strawberry, but doubtless he never did." I want to paraphrase that statement and say, "Doubtless God could make a better fish than the Michigan grayling, but doubtless he never did."

There are fishes of more brilliant coloring, but none surpass in beauty the peacock of its great dorsal fin and the rose pink of its caudal fin. None have a more graceful shape with lines trim and adapted to glide through the water with great ease. Its dorsal fin is very large and its caudal fin of good proportions.

My experience has taught me that ounce for ounce in weight, the grayling will try your tackle one-half more than the brook trout or any other Michigan fish, with the possible exception of the black bass. If you get one on your line in the swift waters of the Au Sable, you will be fortunate as well as skillful if you land your fish, for the grayling is a tender mouthed fish and you must exercise your greatest care and skill in handling him. One of our great authorities disputes this and says that it is not more tender mouthed than most other fish, but my experience disagrees with his statement

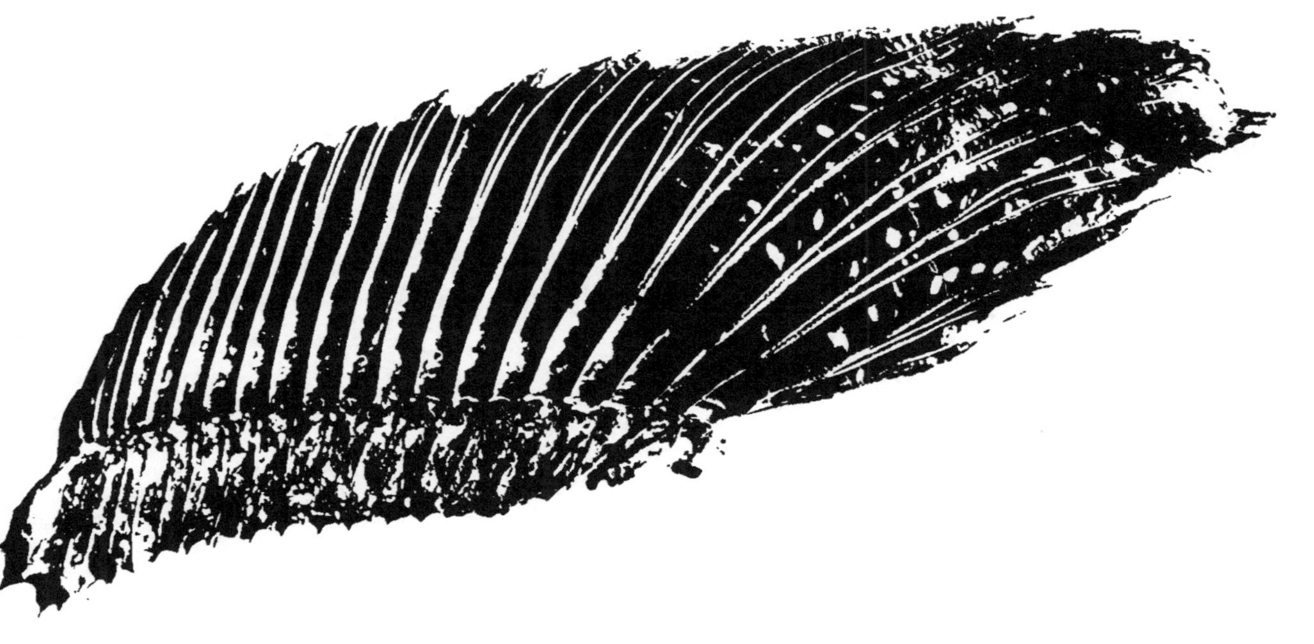

DORSAL FIN OF MICHIGAN GRAYLING.

"THYMALLUS TRICOLOR"

This fish was 18½ inches long, and was taken on artificial fly from Little Manistee River in 1888, by F. L. Borden, of Saginaw, Mich.

and everyone who has had experience in catching the grayling in the Au Sable and Manistee states that it is a very tender mouthed fish. The weight of authority agrees with me on this point.

I have fished the Manistee and Au Sable many times each year from 1876, when it was virgin water, and I believe I know considerable about this fine fish. The meat is a pure white, resembling the whitefish more than any other fish I am acquainted with. It is delicious in flavor and suits my taste better than any other fish I have ever eaten. To be appreciated it should be cooked and eaten as soon as possibile after it is taken from the water.

The grayling is a moody fish. Generally it will take the fly or bait as quickly as it is presented, whether you are in sight of the fish or not; the motion of the angler does not seem to frighten or even annoy it, but at times for two or three days in succession it would not take either fly or bait. At such times I have cast my most alluring flies and even rubbed their noses with angle worms, but in vain; I could not tempt them to raise or bite. But when it was in the mood, it would take the flies very freely. We used to fish with three, and some, with four flies attached to the leader, and catches of three or four at a cast were not infrequent. I once caught twelve grayling at five successive casts; mind I say casts, making two triple catches and three double catches. I would not mention this, but that it leads to an important conclusion, to wit: That the grayling probably could not withstand the excessive fishing which its native waters have undergone, because of its greediness.

I, as well as all others who enjoyed the grayling fishing in the olden days, very much regret its disappearance, and sometimes say, "I wish the trout had never been planted in the Au Sable and the stream reserved for the grayling alone." This is a very natural feeling, but I am inclined to the opinion that even if the trout had not been introduced, the grayling would have disappeared or at least become very scarce, and its cold waters would be furnishing very little sport as compared with what it does at present. We are forced to the conclusion that the present condition of our streams produce the greatest good to the greatest number, though at a great price, namely, the loss of the grayling.

This leads up to the question of the causes of the disappearance of the grayling in the Lower Peninsula of Michigan. We must recollect that the grayling is a spring spawner, that it spawns on the gravel where it lies the year round, as it is emphatically a local fish and does not run upstream or up the small rills and brooks to spawn. This has caused many to say that the log driving, which occurred during the spawning season of the grayling, was the cause of its disappearance since it covered up with soil and debris the eggs. I know from personal experience that the log driving did decrease the number of fish in the Au Sable and in the Manistee. But I also know from personal experience that after the log driving was finished the grayling increased in both streams and the fishing became good again.

We must recollect that the grayling inhabited the swift waters of the streams, so much so, that in the olden days when we came to still water we ceased to cast our flies and did not again resume until we again reached swift waters. There were no cannibal fish in the grayling streams except the pike, and the pike is an inhabitant of lakes, ponds and the still waters of the rivers and consequently was not destructive to the grayling.

The grayling fishing remained good and increased until sometime after we found the brook trout and the rainbow trout in the streams where they had been planted in the Au Sable and the Manistee. In the olden days we frequently caught small grayling from two and one half to four inches long in the fall, they being the hatch of that year's spring spawning.

After the trout, both brook and rainbow, became more plentiful we noticed a scarcity of the catch of the small grayling in the fall. Then we began to notice that the catch of grayling while much fewer in number, were much larger in size, until the last few years during which an occasional grayling was taken, we caught none but mature fish, and the brook and rainbow trout increased greatly in number and size. When we remember that the trout inhabits the swift waters and is as great a cannibal as any fish that lives, it seems to be demonstrated that the actual cause of the disappearance of the grayling was due to the trout eating, first, the fry and then the small grayling, and that those persons who believe that the log driving was responsible for the disappearance of the grayling are mistaken. Some even state that the grayling and the trout will live and increase in the same waters. I am convinced that this is an error. I know that they did live together for a time and I have frequently caught a trout and grayling at the same cast, but this did not last but a short time, before the grayling entirely disappeared.

It is also a fact that my friend, Mr. Wm. B. Mershon, and also Mr. T. E. Douglas have introduced into the waters of the North Branch of the Au Sable the fry of the Montana grayling, and it is also a fact that none of them have ever been heard from. I am forced to the conclusion that the fry planted have been of no use except as food for the trout in the stream where fry were planted.

It throws some light on the subject when we recall that the European brown trout was a number of years ago planted in the Au Sable and Manistee and that they are now very numerous and that the brook trout and the rainbow are becoming fewer. We know that the European brown trout is a great cannibal and grows to a weight of twelve pounds and over, and that it feeds upon all kinds of trout, and it seems very plain that the brown trout will gradually cause the other trout to disappear, and I venture the prediction that in the next fifteen or twenty years the brook and rainbow will have disappeared.

MICHIGAN GRAYLING. (Thymallus Tricolor.)

I am very sorry to have to believe this and sincerely hope that I am mistaken, but I have great fear for the future of the brook and rainbow trout in the Au Sable and Manistee. This will be a great misfortune if it comes because the brown trout is not the equal of the others either as furnishing good sport or food. It is only another example of the folly of our people in importing fish and birds from the other continent with disastrous results, as witness the introduction of the English sparrow, which has driven out our eaves swallows from their old habitat to the great injury of our orchards which the swallows greatly benefited by the destruction of the many insects upon which they fed.

Eheu and vale, my old friend the Michigan grayling: I shall never again see you or your equal.

GEORGE L. ALEXANDER.

Grayling, Michigan, Feb. 13th, 1923.

Extract from Transactions of Michigan Sportsman's Association 1878, Battle Creek, Michigan. Article by L. D. Norris, Grand Rapids, Michigan

"THE MICHIGAN GRAYLING. WHAT MUST BE DONE TO PREVENT THE ANNIHILATION OF THIS EXCELLENT FOOD AND GAME FISH."

"Mr. President and Gentlemen of the Michigan Sportsman's Association:—

I was indebted to Mr. Fitzhugh's generous courtesy and coaching for my first experimental knowledge of the haunts and habits, in the sunny ripples and cool shadows of the Sable, of this aristocrat of game fish—Michigan's grayling; and some generous indignation we exchanged over its annual slaughter and rapid disappearance, doubtless led to his request that I should say on paper that which was so freely uttered over sundry glasses of whiskey-sour, taken, to be sure, as a medicinal corrective to a two weeks' exclusive diet of grayling and bacon, served in the green shadow of the Sable cedar by that master of the setting-pole and 'jewell' of a woods-cook, 'Len,' the guide, philosopher and friend.

"A middle-aged man's first love is apt to be violent—which may account for the opinions that follow. Of all the fresh water game fish, the grayling is, as centuries ago the French found him in Lake Leman, 'un chevalier,' just as certain as the chub is 'un villian.'

"His is no new family. Before the days of the 'Gentle Isaak' under the name of umber (ombre) he passed like a shadow or a ghost out of sight in the clear and cold streams of Switzerland and la belle France.

"Much quaint learning and fanciful discourse have been had anent him. That he fed on gold and grains of it were found in his belly; that he loves the water Thyme (hence thymallus) and smells of it, a habit that he keeps up in the Sable, as I have discovered leaves of white cedar in his breakfast, albeit he might have risen to and taken it, thinking it something more nutritious.

"Aldrovandus says, 'they are made by their Mother Nature of such exact shape and pleasant colors, purposely to invite us to a joy and contentedness in feasting with her' and that they are very 'medicinable.' Gesner notes 'that the fat of a grayling, being set with honey, a day or two in the sun in a little glass, is very excellent against redness or swarthiness, or anything that breeds in the eyes.'

"St. Ambrose of Milan, who kept the church fast days, calls him the 'Flower Fish,' and was so far in love with him that he would not let him pass without the honor of a long discourse. Old Isaak, who tells this of the saint, adds, 'but I must,' yet he tarries long enough with him to leave to us, as he wrote it, more than two centuries ago, an accurate description of Michigan's grayling as I found him in the year of 'Boss' government, 1877.

" 'The biggest of them do not exceed eighteen inches, is very gamesome at the fly and bites not often at the minnow; is much simpler than the trout and therefore bolder, for he will rise twenty times if you miss him, and yet rise again. He is taken with a fly of red feathers (I found he hankered after the 'grass widow' most), an outlandish bird, and a fly like a great or small moth. He lurks close all winter, but is pleasant and jolly after mid April, and in May and the hot months. He is of fine shape and his flesh is white; his teeth, those little ones that he hath, are in the throat, and yet he has so tender a mouth that he is oftener lost after an angler has hooked him than any other fish.

"That he has so tender a mouth and is so often lost after he is struck is one of his chief merits to the true disciple of the quaint old 'semster.' And then too, like the blue-blooded Princes of Europe, he has no end of learned names—cuss names 'Len' calls them—as O'Connell put to rout the Billingsgate fish-wife with the epithets rhomboidal and tetragonal.

"Linnaeus, Cuvier, Heckel, Kner, Richardson, Agassiz, Milner and Cope have all baptised his tribe, or some family of it, with Latin words of learned length and thundering sound. Yet he is just as sweet a 'Flower Fish' under his Equimau disguise of 'Hewlook Powak' or the voyageur's 'Poison bleu,' as the learned Salmo, Coregonus, and Thymallus of the savants.

"His American history seems to be this: Dr. Richardson first took him, 17½ inches long, in 1820 in Winter River, opposite Fort Enterprise, finding him only in the clear water, delighting only in the most rapid part of the stream, and requiring as much skill in landing as a trout of six times his weight. In 1859 he was thought not to be found south of the 62d parallel, but it is now made to appear that before that he had been killed by British army officers in the waters of Hudson Bay, while thirty years ago he was speared by fishermen at the mouth of the Sable, but was not known as a game fish nor classed. In 1865 Mr. Fitzhugh sent a specimen to the Academy of Natural

Science at Philadelphia, and Cope christened him Thymallus tricolor, which is now his ruling Michigan name; though I like best the one Agassiz gives him, Thy: Vexillifer—Thyme-smelling banner-carrier. It alone fitly designates that magnificent dorsal of twenty-three rays, of blackish-gray, blotched with white, crossed by Berlin blue spots, and edged with light lake, which he spreads and waves and fights with, as he comes broadside to your fish-well, under the gentle leading of an eight ounce rod (mine, by the way, was a much heavier one—for lending—as well as my wrist, weak from long disuse, doth yet remember.)

"In 1867 Spencer of the U. S. A. found and described him in Montana. He is in the Yukon, Alaska. The genial Genio C. Scott first hears of him in '68 and learns, which is true, that he is the swiftest fresh water fish that swims. While Hallock of the "Forest and Stream" knows more of him than any other of the tide (the t almost slipped into an h) bound fishermen of the Atlantic coast.

"His only habitat, for the average sportsman, is north of Thunder Bay and in Michigan, and he can only be found in great numbers in the middle and lower Sable and the upper half of the Manistee. He stops with his family on the spawning beds in winter, leaving numerous eggs which hatch in about two weeks in April.

"I know of but one attempt to cultivate him. April 30th, '74, Seth Green was on the Sable for spawn, but was too late and got but little. He found the water to be about 40° Farenheit and the air 20°. His calendar of what did hatch is as follows:

" 'Eggs arrive May 5th; 1st eggs hatched May 8th; all hatched May 11th; first began to rise and eat May 12th; all swimming May 15.'

"Though Mr. Green thought they would not live in the same streams with trout, and that trout would eat them, our Fish Commission in their report of December 1874, say they have kept sixteen grayling, from six to fourteen inches, at Pokagon for the last nine months with several hundred trout as a happy family.

"It is time to come to my text—if one ever does notice it after it is taken.

"It is now but a few years (since '73) that these noble fish could be taken in large quantities at Grayling, a station on the J. L. & S. R. R., where the fisherman first strikes the middle branch of the Sable; now there are none to speak of nearer than twenty miles by land and forty miles by river. They mostly abound within five miles of the confluence of the north and south branches. I found the largest I killed—17 inches and not quite two ounces to the inch—about a mile up the south branch. Yet they are here not out of reach of slaughter, for while I was on the river in August last two large camps, all non-residents and strangers (in old Roman times the word meant enemies) killed five thousand fish, not going beyond five miles of the mouth of the north branch. They salted and carried away at least half of them. Many were eaten, more were wasted. For two miles below from their camps decaying fish whitened the stream, and the offal and fish entrails left unburied in camp tainted the air, as the dead fish poisoned the water. Now when it is remembered that a salted grayling is more tasteless and worthless than so many salted chips, and that these fish were carried away, not for food, but only because of senseless strife—that one party might outdo the other and furnish visible evidence that they had not magnified the magnitude of their catch, it will readily be seen how unsportsmanlike and wicked is such wholesale slaughter.

"True, every fish they caught cost them from first to last at least ten cents, but it was a summer frolic of thoughtless business men—not sportsmen, to whom money was no consideration. The rule on the river, which the guides and polers try to enforce, is to put back all fish below ten inches, yet in the strife between five or six boats as to who shall bring to the fish-pen the greatest number, the rule is disregarded and they take the benefit of a doubt—down to six or seven inches.

"While on the river last August I took quite a number of salmon of seven, eight and nine inches, fine healthy, growing fish (the plant of our Fish Commission) and was always careful to put them tenderly back. The parties I speak of were not so careful. Many were killed and went into the salt. No stream will long survive such treatment.

"It is—for the State—killing the goose that lays the golden eggs. Each year, as the delicate beauty and gameness of this delicious fish becomes wider known, brings a greater number of honest fishermen from abroad, who come for sport, and not indiscriminate and senseless slaughter. These add to the reputation of the State, leave money in our borders, and advertise widely our fourteen hundred miles of water coast and 35,000 square miles of fish-breeding water.

"Now what is the remedy? It is difficult to prescribe a proper one. Some further legislation is needed—greater powers ought to be conferred on and more money put at the disposal of our Fish Commissioners. In the case of the parties I refer to, a printed circular giving rules for fishing the river, issued by the Commission and put in their hands, I am sure would be respected. They were gentlemen, though thoughtless ones. These circulars could easily be distributed. They would certainly be by guides and polers, for however well they are paid, they do not care to destroy in one year the livelihood of three, and work from daylight to dark, coming in wet and weary—if they might avoid it. For those who can not be so reached more stringent laws should be enacted, with penalties heavy enough to tempt informers. And the moulding of such legislation is the proper duty of the Fish Commission.

"Our oldest fish laws are comparatively recent (1865), though antedating by four years the game law proper (1869). These laws, however, are in some respects discordant and incomplete. They need codifying, enlarging and amending. Still the progress has been steady, and I desire to add here my warmest thanks to the Fish Commission for the zeal and efficiency with which they have worked and husbanded the pittance doled out to them. One has but to read the legislation of '73, '75 and '77 to note this steady progress in a good cause, to which your Association has largely contributed.

"More and more attention is being given to the preservation and culture of fish by our sister states. At least eighteen of them have Fish Commissioners and favoring legislation. And yet not one of them can approach Michigan in the magnitude of its undeveloped resources in this regard. Whether the grayling can become by culture a food fish is yet a problem. He is, however, the peculiar property of Michigan waters, and is fast growing into favor with the best class of our many men of leisure, who love the rod and fly and the quiet woods. And let it be remembered that the friends of trout and grayling—and their name is legion—are always found in the front ranks of these, who with money and culture and influence and zeal, are laboring to hold up the hands of our Fish Commission and educate the State to a proper appreciation of the wealth of the waters of our beautiful peninsula."

Grand Rapids, Feb. 5, 1878.

Paper Written by Mr. Fred Mather Read Before the Michigan Sportsman's Association at Bay City, Michigan, February 3rd, 1880

The Committee on Fish Laws (including propagation as well as protection) reported a paper by Mr.

Fred Mather, which was read by Mr. Colburn, one of the Committee, as follows:

"A Few Words on Fish Propagation and Protection" by Fred Mather

"To the Michigan Sportsman's Association:

Gentlemen:

Lest it should be thought by some that an outsider is making himself "too numerous," or as others more classically express it "too fresh," which might be translated into the transient slang of the day as too officious, in addressing your Honorable Body, I will offer the following apology:

Should you ask me why these warnings,
Why these statements and petitions,
With the flavor of the stream-side,
With the curling smoke of camp-fire,
With the damp of hatching-houses;
From a dweller in New Jersey
To your State Association?
I should answer, I should tell you:

"From the forests and the prairies,
From the Great Lakes of the Northland,
Down the noble Mississippi,
Where the musky alligator
Feeds among the Florida marshes,

DORSAL FIN OF MICHIGAN GRAYLING

Taken from a fish weighing 1½ lbs. Note how far this fin projected in the rear from point of attachment. The spots were violet and vermilion, transparent.

And from Maine to California,
Just now stocked with smiling catfish—
All this land is mine to live in,
Mine to shoot in, mine to fish in,
Mine to hatch and catch the fish in,
For I hold no State allegiance,
And my thought is never fettered
My affections never hampered
By the small and narrow State lines,
Which the local politician
Sets as fences, rears as hedges,
To prevent his dwarfed opinions
Wandering far among the big fish,
Lest they stray and he should lose them.

I should answer, I should tell you,
From the lakes of your Peninsula,
Where the savage pike, kenozha,
And the mighty sturgeon, namah,
Dwell at peace within the waters,
To that farther south peninsula,
To that southern land of flowers,
Where the melancholy "cracker"
Skins his northern winter visitor,
Sells him teeth of alligator
Made from bone of hog, or deer horn.

Of all this broad and fruitful country,
I am native, I am citizen,

And the name which I rejoice in,
Which I revel and delight in,
Is, that I am
An
AMERICAN.

The general interest which I take in the subject of fish propagation and protection in all parts of our country is, in my opinion, sufficient reason to ask attention to this paper by all who take such an interest. Fish culture in Michigan is capable of great results; it has an able Fish Commission, and it has a State Sportsman's Association of which any State might well be proud, whose main object is not the slaughter of pigeons, but the protection of its furred, finned and feathered game.

In a recent article in the Chicago Field I read that there were only three such Associations (all honor to them), the "Cuvier Club" of Cincinnati, the New Hampshire, and the Michigan, who were, in fact, what their names imply—associations for the protection of game. In other States this is so notoriously the reverse that their meeting is always spoken of as "the State shoot;" truth, if not grammar.

It is not to be expected that a sportsmen's association will take up the question of fish protection and propagation in its broader sense of including all the commercial fishes and such food fishes as do not take the hook, nor is it to be desired, as the Fish Commission has these things directly in charge; but, as an adjunct to that

Commission, there is much good to be done both in influencing the needed legislation and in educating the people as to what is necessary to be done in order to preserve what they have, and to restore the depleted waters to fruitfulness. Leaving out the lake fishes, let us consider two species whose commercial value is small in comparison to the others, but which afford a great amount of health-giving sport to your people, and bring tourists to your State to angle for them, who leave in cash ten times their marketable value. Can your people then afford to let these fish be speared and netted for market by the poacher? Can they afford to have them caught during the spawning season, and the seed for the future destroyed? Can they afford to have these trout and grayling replaced by meaner fish?

The streams in the northern portion of the settled part of your State are peculiarly adapted to these two fish; those like the Au Sable flowing east into Lake Huron, and west like the Manistee into Lake Michigan, being the natural home of the grayling, while above these the streams which flow northward abound in trout.

The grayling is a fish which fifteen years ago was not known to exist on this continent, except to a few. When its existence was first discovered by anglers, there were great disputes about it, and some in New York who had taken the grayling in England and were supposed to know and be able to identify it, denied that our fish was one of the graylings, while others made themselves ridiculous by calling it a mongrel, a cross between a perch and a sucker, thereby displaying their ignorance of physiological laws, which forbid the crossing of animals structurally different; others denied its value as a food and game fish, an opinion not concurred in by those who know them, as hundreds testify who have made pilgrimages to your state to take them.

Gentlemen, save the grayling. It is a delicate fish whose limited habitat proves one of two things; either its range has been wider, and it has been gradually driven from all waters, except in the narrow belt across your state by other fishes devouring its food or its young; or it flourishes in its present habitat by reason of the absence of such fishes, and is unable to extend its range by migration into neighboring streams on account of them.

The small mouth of the grayling and its exceedingly fine teeth proclaim it a feeder upon insects and their larvae, and forbid it to prey in turn upon the young of their enemies, hence it would not appear proper to stock their streams with trout, which hatching from December to February, are large enough in April to swallow the young grayling just out of its shell. Another danger to this fish is the running of logs in the spring time, which tears up the gravel beds in which our fish lay their eggs. It would not be a great annoyance to the lumbermen to stop the running of logs during the short time which the grayling are spawning and hatching. This time, as near as I am able to tell it, is, in the Au Sable, from the 1st of April to the 15th of May, but may vary some with the season. In 1874 Mr. D. H.

Fitzhugh, Jr. and myself were on this river April 1st, and the fish had not begun to spawn; business called me hence, and I returned without eggs. Mr. Fitzhugh was on the river again on the 30th, and found the fish had all spawned.

The next year we went to stay, and on the 8th, 9th and 10th of April took many eggs, some of which I took home and hatched. These were all out on the 8th of May, and were feeding a week afterward. Some of the eggs were given to Mr. Clark of Northville, who raised the fish to maturity, a full account of which can be found in the Chicago Field of January 17th, vol. XII., p. 356, which quiets all doubts about raising the grayling in confinement, although it is fair to state that these fish, which were four years old last April, had not yet spawned in Mr. Clark's pond, but one sent alive to the Smithsonian Institute, and afterward to Mr. E. G. Blackford, of Fulton Market, New York, was found to be full of eggs after death last spring.

Whether this fish can be raised in ponds or in other streams, and hold its own with other fishes or not, it can at least be preserved by protection in its native streams, where, being in the ascendancy in point of numbers, it can thrive among the cyprinoids which are already in those rivers, all of which are spawn eaters. If protection against poachers, over fishing and fishing out of season, and the running of logs is supplemented by the aid of the fish culturist, there seems to be no fear of the loss of this fish, which under present influences, is in great danger of becoming extinct, and only to be found in the future bleached out in alcohol in the museums with other animals of a former age.

The splendid trout streams of the upper part of your state also need timely help or they too are doomed; not so soon as the grayling perhaps, for the predaceous habits of the trout place it nearer an equality with its enemies, and if pike devour them or suckers pick their eggs out of the gravel, the young pike and sucker will feel the avenging tooth of the trout and settle for the sins of their parents. Still the same causes which have made barren the streams of the older states, are slowly and surely at work on yours, and if this paper has furnished any facts which may be of value or hints which will cause attention to be called to the danger, then it has not been written in vain. If I have presumed too far in claiming your attention to so long a lecture by an outsider, I can only say that among your number I have warm personal friends who will make all due apologies, and to them I leave the case. Closing with the hope that your good work may meet with a proper appreciation and be backed up by the people at large, for whose interests you are really working without expectation of personal reward."

Paper Read Before The Michigan Sportsman's Association at Bay City, Michigan, February 4th, 1880, by Frank N. Clark, Northville, Michigan

Mr. Frank N. Clark of Northville, a member of the U. S. Fish Commission, read the following paper:

"The Red-Banded Trout of California" (Salmo Iridea)

"Mr. Chairman and Gentlemen of the Association:

In presenting my mite to the Association, I would ask the indulgence of its members while I give a short description of one of the best fishes for both the sportsmen and the people at large. I refer to the red-banded trout of California (Salmo iridea) a fish little known here, but much prized by sporting men on the Pacific slope. In the description given to Prof. Baird, of Washington, by Mr. Livingston Stone, (whom you are all well aware is considered the best of authority for all fishes found in the western waters), he says of this fish: "This trout found in the Little Sacramento and McCloud rivers, is called by the Indians "syoo-lott" or red-banded trout. This band extends the whole length of the body and about as wide as one-fourth the depth of the fish. The band overlies the lateral line and is about evenly divided by it." Mr. Stone claims that the scarlet band is an accidental feature dependent upon seasons and localities, as for instance on the coast it is rarely seen in its full brightness and is so rare that fishermen call it a different variety and esteem it an unusual prize, while in the Lower McCloud the band is visible in June and continues to grow deeper colored till the middle of August, when it entirely disappears and does not show itself in September or October. At the head waters of Sacramento, the golden band is bright the year round, and the trout are very abundant, being easily caught at all seasons of the year with artificial fly or the ordinary trout fishing bait.

This trout, according to my own experience, can be easily domesticated.

If not wearying your patience too much, let me give you a brief description of my efforts in procuring some of them in their native waters. In July '77, I was sent to California by the U. S. Fish Commission with young shad, designed for the Sacramento River. After depositing my charge in their final home at Tehema, about 150 miles north of Sacramento City, from which place I had been accompanied by Mr. Readding, Fish Commissioner of California, and Mr. Stone, they kindly invited me to a day's enjoyment on the McCloud River. On leaving the terminus of the road at Reading, we proceeded by stage a distance of 30 miles to the U. S. Salmon Fishery. The ride in the open air, after the tedium of travel by rail, was a delightful change, and the scenery, like all in California, was wild and grand. Having the pleasure of good company, in addition to the fine surroundings and a pleasant day in prospect, I gave myself up to full enjoyment, leaving dull care behind. About 4.00 o'clock in the morning, we made our first attempt at trout fishing, but had no success till we began baiting them, when we found them a ready prey to our allurements. In this respect I found them different from our native trout, and from all observation, think they could habituate themselves readily to any change. Being very successful in our day's work (or sport we found it), we greatly enjoyed the luscious meal set before us of the trout mentioned. The meat, to an epicure, exhibits a flavor and richness unsurpassed by any other fish, being fine and juicy, and unlike other fish, as they increase in size the quality remains the same. Those caught by us varied in weight from two to four pounds, while they have been found as high as nine pounds.

The following year, while in California, I visited the private ponds of Mr. Chabot of San Leandro, where he had about 10,000 of the red-banded trout in a temperature of 68°. He was very desirous of my undertaking to transport some to Michigan, but I greatly feared it would result in much loss, but consented, provided he would allow me to sort out the smallest among several thousand. We could not find any less than from five to seven inches in length.

I took one hundred and twenty-five of these, and at his earnest request, also took twenty-five of the largest, which were from ten to eleven and a half inches in length. These were all yearlings, and he was anxious some of the large ones should be brought here also.

I started from San Leandro with this trust on July 1st, with the young trout in water at a temperature of 68°. with no ice, and before reaching Sacramento City it had reached 75° The small fish were in four cans, holding 15 gallons to the can. The twenty-five large ones were in two cans of the same size. I had no difficulty in bringing the small trout safely, with a varying temperature, but lost most of the larger ones from a fungus growth, caused by their injuring themselves against the cans. The trout were all of the red-banded variety and there has been no change in their color since placing them in the spring water at my hatchery. Allow me, in addition, to say that of the number successfully landed here, I planted about twenty-five in one of the streams tributary to the River Rouge, near my hatchery, and have since caught some of them after a year's isolation from their mates, and found their growth equal to the others reared artificially, showing conclusively that they will live in our waters. The method of procuring and caring for the eggs artificially, is of course similar to the salmon. But while the fish are in the fry state, they require very little care compared with our trout. One subject that should receive due notice by fish culturists is the difference between the "Salmo iridea" and "Salmo Fontanalis" in the manner of securing their food. All who have bred the brook trout, know that as a rule they will not pick up their food after it has once fallen to the bottom of the pond, but take it in transit; also, that if fed more than required, the refuse contaminates the water and must be removed in order to keep the fish in a healthy condition, while the California trout will gather their food as they require it and will not be injured by an over supply in the water.

Therefore, compared with our native trout, I consider them more hardy, easier to acclimate, and from personal observation, more rapid growers. While I prize our own fish highly, at the same time it looks reasonable that this variety will prove far superior and more economical for the mass of the people. As the California salmon has been planted in many of our streams all over the country and much time and money expended in the experiment, why not, in connection with this effort, add the California trout? I conscientiously believe that with a little intelligence and energy on this interesting subject, much might be accomplished for our benefit.

Would it not be advisable for our State Commission to investigate this matter and give it a thorough trial, thus adding to our list a variety of fish that I believe would tempt the sportsman and the epicure, while in course of time it might become a source of profit."

An interesting discussion followed, in which many questions were asked by the members in regard to the superb game fish referred to in Mr. Clark's paper, and which elicited the facts that the red-banded trout was a hardy fish, very prolific in breeding, more gamey than the Michigan grayling (Thymalus signifer), of large size and delicious flavor.

Salmon Fishing

IN 1886 I first went to the Grand Cascapedia River, Province of Quebec, salmon fishing. As I look back now it is very strange compared to the present time. Then a half dozen of us arrived for the month of July, having rented the fishing of the late R. G. Dun, which consisted of the Shedden Pool at Woodman's and all of the water above it on the eastern side facing Lorne cottage. I think this included the Little Curley, Titus Nest, and I am sure the Princess Pool. Then down the river was a long stretch of the Salmon Hole.

We all stayed at Woodman's. There were three sisters then that managed the household affairs and we were beautifully taken care of, and there was a jolly party of us—Lowry, Deacon White, then in the heyday of his stock market glory, Mr. Payne, afterwards Bank Commissioner of the state of New York, Mr. Bigelow of Boston, General Jackson of the English Army who was then living with a married son or daughter at Oakville, Ont., and H. P. Wells, who wrote such delightful books on fishing, and from whom I learned the proper way to cast a salmon rod. There were so many of us that we had to fish turn about; one would fish in the morning and another in the afternoon, the morning fisherman lying off or going in the boat as a visitor without a rod. We were all a lot younger and had worlds of fun besides fishing.

Leases of salmon water were obtained at ridiculously low prices. I think the Harrison-Moen Pools were at that time under lease to Mr. Skelton of Montreal, and he didn't pay to exceed $10.00 to $15.00 a year for either one. Soon after that Milligan wanted to sell his side of the Salmon Hole, which was the entire western side and a long stretch above it. It didn't bring much, if any, above $2,000. That was for the land and salmon fishing, and if I am not mistaken, a pretty good sized barn on the property. There were mighty few salmon pools that brought over $15.00 to $25.00 a year.

Skelton invited me to an afternoon's fishing at the Harrison and I had good luck. Then Lowry and I began making some leases. No water had ever been under lease on the Northwest Branch and we leased some frontage of Cormier and it was named the Lowry Pool. I recall getting two very fine 28-lb. salmon in there one afternoon—the very first salmon I had ever taken, for the first year when we were at Woodman's I did not get a fish, but did have most excellent sea trout fishing. The largest sea trout I ever took in the Cascapedia weighed 7¾ lbs. They are brook trout, no different from those of New England except that they have gone to salt water for food and grown enormously in consequence.

We moved down to Peter Barter's after the first two years at Woodman's and eventually Lowry and I acquired considerable salmon water by lease and purchase, so that we continued salmon fishing together for some years.

Mr. Lowry sold his interest in our fishing to the late R. W. Paterson and later on Mr. Paterson retired and I purchased it. I built Cascapedia Cottage in 1894. It was completed just in time for the arrival of Mrs. Mershon and myself early in June of that year.

I don't intend to write much about salmon fishing for it is a subject by itself and I can not do it justice, but am just giving a few instances that come to my memory now, which because of being unusual are fixed there.

The largest fish I ever killed on the Grand Cascapedia weighed 46 lbs. I have had three weighing 43 lbs. each, and a number ranging from 40 lbs. to 42 lbs. I took thirteen consecutive salmon once that averaged 30 2/3 lbs.

Salmon do queer things. I was on the Junction Pool one day when it was apparently full of fish. They were jumping everywhere, yet try as I could, I could not get one of them to look at my fly. I was fishing over one that had risen a little while before when one jumped just below. I dropped and tried for him but it was no use. I changed the flies as to color and size and method of fishing. Finally I put on a medium sized fly (my recollection is it was a Thunder and Lightning, about a 1/0 single hook) but I don't think the fly had anything to do with it. I shortened the line so it was not much longer than the rod and began dancing the fly on top of the water just as if it was jumping up and down and alighting on the water. Mind you, this was at a place where I had fished for sometime over this very same fish, that now with a rush came clear out of the water his whole length, grabbed the fly, and after a lively fight, I boated a fresh run salmon weighing 26 lbs.

Another time I was fishing Little Curley. A trout seven or eight inches long had taken my salmon fly and I was reeling it in when a salmon followed this trout and kept nipping it and biting it until it came very close to the boat. This salmon must have nipped the trout I was reeling in a half dozen times at least.

The greatest number of times I ever had a salmon jump was sixteen. These were leaps after the fish was hooked. Ordinarily about three is the limit. Salmon like to chase a fly that is being drawn away from it. They are a good deal like a dog that will chase a person if he runs away, and the minute the person stops the dog stops. I have watched salmon in clear water doing the same thing. As long as you keep the fly moving away from them they will go after it, and finally work up courage enough to grab it.

I took a salmon once that weighed 8 lbs. on a 5 oz. trout rod with a No. 8 Professor trout fly. This fish evidently was feeding. It was in shallow water. I thought it was a large trout and after fishing the Pool, moved over and cast for this supposedly large trout. It proved to be a salmon. On opening it, remains of flies and bugs were found within it, but in such a state

I could not be sure that they were recently taken into the stomach.

Once when salmon were rising and taking freely, I hooked a fish and on striking it, the fish being at the surface, the fly popped out of his mouth. It struck the water some twenty or thirty feet to one side, and the instant the fly hit the water another fish grabbed it, which I played and successfully boated.

Another strange thing in connection with salmon fishing. A few years ago my friend, W J. Hunsaker of Saginaw, Michigan, at that time President of the Michigan State Fish Commission, was my guest and fishing the Moen Pool. Alexander Barter was his head guide. He hooked a good sized salmon and in some way it ran through a wire barrel hoop that must have been lying between the stones, cocked up in some way so that the fish could get through it. The salmon jumped, and the line brought to the surface the barrel hoop, much to the surprise of my friend and his canoeman. They couldn't figure out what it was or what was the trouble. There was a long awkward fight, and when the fish was finally brought near enough to the boat to gaff, it was easily seen what the trouble was. There was the barrel hoop riding the line and it proved the undoing of the gaffer, for in striking at his fish, he somehow or other hit the hoop and it broke the leader and the fish got away. Afterwards it was easy enough to figure out how they could have lifted the wire hoop with the gaff and slipped it over the rod, but that was an afterthought and came too late, but how under the sun that salmon picked out the barrel hoop as a place of refuge is one of the salmon mysteries.

Unquestionably salmon angling is grand sport, but it has not spoiled me for my trout fishing. There is a charm about wading a trout stream and daintily casting your small fly with the finest of tackle which has a fascination so distinct and different from salmon fishing that one does not detract from or interfere with the other in the least.

A Sketch Relating to Mr. David C. Sanborn and to His Llewellin Setter Dog Count Noble

MICHIGAN has always been a wonderful field for the propagation of game birds such as the ruffed grouse, quail, woodcock, snipe, duck, etc., and the use of the bird hunting dog has added very much to the pleasure of the wing shooting sportsman in following this feathered game.

Originally the native dogs of bird hunting type were rather coarse of structure and performance, but the plentifulness of game was such that refinement in these directions was not so very necessary. The development of the wing shooting sport here and in other game bearing states was such that considerable attention was being given to the breeding and training of setters and pointers. This was much accelerated by such gifted sportsmen as Henry William Herbert (Frank Forester) who in his charming booklets of "Warwick Woodlands," the "Shooting Box," and like delicious hunting stories, descriptive of the open life in the field with dog and gun, gave much pleasure and added interest to the oncoming lover of field sports.

It was in these times, along in 1860, that Mr. David C. Sanborn, then of Seabrook, N. H., came to Battle

DAVID C. SANBORN

Creek, Michigan, bringing with him a well-bred old pointer dog, then about the only bird dog in our locality. Mr. Sanborn started in the banking business in Battle Creek, but failing health induced him to buy a farm in the town of Baltimore, Barry County, about fifteen miles away, where he took up for recreation and pleasure the breeding, training, handling and developing of English setter dogs.

He met with great success in his early exhibits of setters which he raised, trained and exhibited at various kennel shows and field trails and his success in these lines was given much publicity by notable sporting papers such as Forest and Stream, Chicago American Field, and others.

There was in England great strife among the wealthy and aristocratic breeders of bird dogs such as the Laverack, the Gordon, the Scotch, the Irish and others. Among them was R. Ll. Purcell-Llewellin, breeder of the Llewellin type. Mr. Llewellin was a notable prize winner with his dogs, but he never sold one and probably none were in this country. His kennel master, Mr. Buckell, learning of Mr. Sanborn's great success as a trainer, exhibitor and handler in field trials over here, made him a present of a Llewellin puppy dog, which he shipped to Mr. Sanborn in 1880. This was the famous Llewellin setter, Count Noble, which Mr. Sanborn trained, developed and exhibited in field trials with astonishing success. Count Noble is not so noted for his prize winnings, being placed but four times in field trials, but for his prepotency as a sire, a majority of the great setters of the present day tracing back to him. This includes such world winners as Gath, Cincinnatus, Roderigo, Prince Noble, Antonio, Sweetheart, Lily Borgess, Janet, Katie Noble, Cassio, Bohemian Girl, Dashing Noble, Count Gladstone IV, Eugene T. Lady's Count Gladstone, Tony Boy, and Count Gladstone, and scores of other notables, whose records of great performance were fully noted in the sporting papers of the time.

The chief characteristics of Sanborn's Count Noble in action which were so largely transmitted to his progeny were extreme high speed with a high head, swinging tail, fine style, great action, and great endurance, together with an extraordinary keenness of nose that permitted him to discard the foot scent and with high up head, take the body scent instead, enabling him to "nail" his points with most beautiful certainty and protection against over-running or flushing. His ability thus to locate his bird at good distance and to flash into his point at his great speed with accuracy and safety was the admiration of every beholder.

The breed of bird hunting dogs was thus greatly improved in fineness of nose and beauty and style of action, all so dear and important to the heart of the true sportsman who enjoys the companionship of this most noble and intelligent specimen of animal life as is the present bird hunting dog of America. Mr. Sanborn's great contribution to the stock of royal pedigreed

COUNT NOBLE, N. A. K. C. S. B., 1509, by Count Windem — Nora

Raised, Trained and Owned by David C. Sanborn, Baltimore Twp., Barry County, Michigan

bird hunting dogs of this country has been generally acknowledged and appreciated by the lovers of hunting dogs and field sports.

EDWIN C. NICHOLS.
Battle Creek, Michigan.

(Mr. Nichols has written to me that he went to the express office to help Mr. Sanborn uncrate Count Noble when he arrived.—W B. M.)

What follows under the title of "The Pilgrimage of the Saginaw Crowd" is a reprint from Forest and Stream of a trip taken during the autumn of 1887, and it ran through four issues of Forest and Stream.

I have hesitated to reproduce this, but it shows how plentiful game, especially wild turkeys, was in the Indian Territory in 1887, and furthermore, my friend, the late Emerson Hough, advised me to use it, for I had a long visit with him in his office about a month before he passed away, at which time he told me that he had planned to write a book of reminiscences of his life in the outdoors. This story was written when I was a young man. There is a lot of difference between one's viewpoint and ability to express it at thirty years compared with sixty-eight.

Pilgrimage of the Saginaw Crowd

I

IT IS usually expected that some member of a party which takes two or three weeks' outing shall be the scribe and chronicler, and report to the Forest and Stream the doings and incidents of the trip. Now, this time I propose to make the other boys turn in and do their share; in other words, kind of act as an editor of the case, which will give readers an opportunity to compare the styles of the different authors, and they will be at liberty in the future to call upon whichever one they consider slings the raciest pen and puts the most hairbreadth escapes and blood-curdling scenes with a realistic effect into his part of the narrative.

It is the old Dakota goose party that I am about to stir up. The readers of the Forest and Stream will remember that it has been the custom of a certain eight boon companions to each year take the good car "City of Saginaw," which belongs to the Saginaw Hunting Club, and make a pilgrimage to some far off land, for the sole and only purpose of having a thoroughly good time. This good time, of course, consisted of as much shooting as we could get, breathing in the pure air of the western prairies to the end that our doctor bills might be less, and last but not the least of the enjoyment was the planning for months beforehand what we should take and where we should go, what we would do after we got there, and when we would start, and the getting together every few nights in the last weeks just before going, to make our plans and talk over the good times we had the year before and were going to have this year. And it did not end here, for after our return there was the same old enthusiasm manifested when any two of the party got together, and one would recall an extra long shot that so-and-so made, or what a delightful time we had the day we went down to the McGuire farm, or the time the undersigned left his gun at the car and did not discover it until the decoys were all placed and the geese coming up through the fog of the early morning, and how the team was despatched to the station nearby to telegraph back to the car to one of the lazy ones, who failed to get up in the morning to go with us, to hire someone to bring the gun with all speed, as it promised to be a great day, and how at last the gun did arrive; how the other boys had had their big shoot, and finally the day was ended with a score of 163 geese, all we could carry in the wagon, and we drove back to the good old car in the dusk of evening, wet, cold and shivering, but happy, and how good the hot lemonade tasted that the City Official had brewed for our coming, knowing by the storm that had raged all the afternoon that we would need something of the kind to cheer up our spirits. Oh, well, I say this part of the trip is not to be despised. Then the comparing of notes; and I don't know, after all, but that anticipation is half of the enjoyment of a sportsman's life.

But this time, instead of Dakota, the trip was to the Indian Territory. We wanted to go to Dakota and were homesick for the spot that for four successive years had been our paradise, but the new game laws prohibited bringing home to our friends much of the game we might kill, and as there were very few inhabitants in the locality where we did most of our shooting, it was impossible to give our birds away or make proper use of them, and of course we did not want to kill anything we could not use. Therefore, when Ed proposed that we go to the Territory and visit their cattle ranch we acquiesced. The Saginaw Cattle Company have 200,000 acres of land fenced in the Sac and Fox Reservation, and we were very glad to go and see how the cattle looked and besides we had reports of plenty of birds. In looking over the old crowd two or three faces were missing. There was the General, whom we had not heard from since we were salmon fishing in the summer, and Bob wrote us that rheumatism prevented his going. "Whisky Bill" of Dakota fame, was somewhere in Kentucky buying fast horses, so they had narrowed down to Ed, the City Official, "Genial George" and Brooks or "Section 37," as he is familiarly called, and the Doctor, together with the writer of this chronicle, whom the boys nicknamed "Buzzard Bill," and undoubtedly the cause of the name will come out later on. So it came to pass that the F. & P. M. train, leaving Saginaw at 8.30 the evening of Oct. 11th bore us toward Chicago. All were present and accounted for with the exception of the Doctor who was to meet us in Chicago in the morning. Our connection with the Wabash was very close, and the Grand Trunk is noted for being late. We had arranged, however, with the traveling passenger agent to hold his train for us if necessary, but somehow or other this did not pan out. It is always thus. You arrange for your transportation with the traveling passenger agent, and he of course guarantees everything, and is to be on hand to see about your transfer, provided you are going in a private car, or he is going to hold the train for you if you are not and it should be necessary to do this in order to make connections, but in all my trips I have never yet had a thing come out just as they agreed. This was no exception, and when we reached the outskirts of Chicago and began crossing the numerous tracks going into the city, waiting for trains here and there, we saw that we were hopelessly late and something must be done. Telegraphing in we found that the Wabash train had not waited for us but that we could possibly catch it by getting off at some junction outside of the city. This we did and our heavy baggage was unloaded, but we were in a peck of trouble to know what we were to do about our transportation, as we merely had orders for tourists' tickets which would be issued us at Chicago. We were going to cheek it through some way as we were not to blame and did not want to be delayed an entire twenty-four hours. Soon the train came rumbling into the station. Somehow the conductor knew about us and was expecting us. The Doctor's cheery face was seen from one of the windows, the dogs were hastily put on board and away we went.

Nothing of importance occurred that day. The dogs were given their exercise at Decatur while the baggage was being transferred from one car to another, and we were there provided with the proper tickets. We had taken precaution to telegraph ahead for our sleeping berths at St. Louis, and it proved to be a very wise precaution as it was the day of the Harvest excursion, besides St. Louis always has some kind of a convention and the town was full of strangers, and when we reached the Union Depot, such a hurrying, scurrying and crowding was never seen. Bells were clanging, women rushing to and fro, dragging helpless children by arms that seemed ready to pull out of the sockets; porters bustled around, stowing away the passengers in the different sleeping cars, and all making ready for the far West. Or those who had been to the land of the setting sun were once more leaving for the cultured East. Around the window of the sleeping car agent was a solid jam of people, twenty deep. There is no rule or system about the different ones taking turns, merely a crush, so that the strongest man rushed in and stood a better show than the poor helpless females with two or three children, who really needed a comfortable lower berth, but nine times out of ten had to take the leavings. Our three sections were waiting for us, and George and Ed had to transfer the dogs and put them to bed for the night, and we were all aboard for the Indian Territory and the West. Here comes in a little something about the peculiarities of baggagemen in making their charges for dogs' transportation. With most railroads there is no charge made for dogs, but it is expected that a gratuity be given the baggageman. Some demand it as a right, while others with more gentlemanly instincts are perfectly willing to "leave it to you, sir" and almost always get a better fee by so doing. The Grand Trunk baggageman roasted us unmercifully, and when we struck the 'Frisco Line they tried to make us believe that dogs were charged half a cent per mile, and began figuring up quite an expense bill on our three. We profited by former experience, however, and got through without much of a robbing. Our sleeper was a new one of the latest pattern and the night was most comfortably passed.

On awakening the next morning we made the acquaintance of a fellow traveler, who was a thorough old Southern gentleman but had acquired the active instincts of the Western land speculator and boomer as well. Slightly helpless from some accident or deformity, he was going accompanied by his servant to the new town of Monet, as he expressed it to "sell out the town." In other words, with the usual enthusiasm created by a brass band and lots of "hoorah," an auction was to be held there that day to dispose of village lots. In due course of time the train pulled into the metropolis. The brass bands were there and so were the village lots, and about as far as the eye could reach there seemed to be lots more lots of the same kind as those that were marked with stakes at each corner, with the exception of price. Those without the mystic talisman of the boundary stakes could undoubtedly be secured at the rate of about $5.00 or $6.00 per acre. But the staked ones, right where the city buildings were to be, and here where the court house was sure to go up, and there where a dry goods store larger than Field's was to be erected—in those places of course land was bound to boom and must be worth several hundred dollars per foot. The depot was new and the surroundings neat and clean, and after getting a good substantial breakfast we exercised the dogs a little by letting them run across some of the city property (and we had a faint suspicion that they started up a rabbit on one of the lots laid out for a public square). As we gave a shrill whistle, and they obediently came in to be tied up, a long, lank individual of the thoroughly Missourian type, witnessing their obedience, rammed his hands down into his pockets a little further, if such a thing were possible, from his teeth ejected about a quart of tobacco juice, and said, "Stranger, them thar dogs 'pear to me to be right bidable." We acquiesced, as we supposed he meant "obedient."

The conductor shouts "All Aboard" and we are once more moving westward, and our next changing place is Vanita, within the limits of the Indian Territory. From the time we had arrived at the depot in Saginaw up to the present time we had heard rumors and stories about how hunters had been fired out of the Territory and that the Secretary of the Interior had given orders to allow no hunting and to confiscate all guns and paraphernalia belonging to the hunters found in the sacred limits. While we supposed this applied to market hunters, or those who made a business of it, and were confident that we would not be molested, as we were going as much on a visiting trip to our friends at the cattle ranch as anything, still some of the boys at times felt uncomfortable and imagined that each stranger looking at us was some government marshal who had nothing to do but spot us. Poor Brooks had brought along some of his cherished medicine in a little flask that was not larger than a good sized hen's egg; inadvertently taking it out of his pocket, happened to catch the eye of a new passenger and immediately surmised that he had broken the law by bringing whisky into the Territory and was bound to be snaked off the train at the next station. So with a very "pale at the gills" expression, he quietly sneaked to the door, and the next minute returned and in a hoarse whisper informed me that he had thrown it away so that they could not find any medicine on his person. We all breathed easier and thought that our lives were saved by his forethought.

Between Monet and Vanita no finer looking ground for quail can be found in the world. Numerous cornfields, with hillsides wooded with scrub oak, little marshes fringed with clumps of heavy weeds, made a most tempting outlook for a sportsman, and we wished for the old car and an extra week's time, that we might devote ourselves to the quail which we were certain were in abundance here. We rumbled into Vanita and were notified to change cars for Red Fork, our train going no farther. Vanita consits of about half a dozen houses and a good deal of dirt and discomfort. The dirt we discovered in some pie and sandwiches we had purchased at the stereotyped railroad eating house. Mose always had a good appetite and was able to eat them, but Bob and Nip have a good deal of common sense and joined us in flatly refusing to partake of the repast, and the consequence was that we went hungry until we had supper with the quiet Mrs. M. at Red Fork. A wheezy old engine with half a dozen freight cars attached, the rear one having three or four old benches stowed in it, was the train that took us toward our journey's end, but the lovely landscape and a perfect day made up for the discomforts of the ride. Probably the finest land in the world, from an agriculturist's standpoint, is to be found in this same Indian Territory. It is neither a wooded nor prairie country, but a mixture of both, and withal is well watered. The larger streams are muddy and sluggish, but any number of small running brooks are to be found in the part of the Territory that we went through, some 150 miles of it. Soon we began to see herds of cattle looking in prime condition, when a sudden vigorous tooting of the engine caused all heads to be stuck out of the windows and door, and we saw the cause was that a large beef critter had disregarded the right of way of the railroad company and was now lying with a broken leg in the ditch alongside. Our hearts were moved with pity for his suffering, as the day was hot and we were told that he would not be killed, but left there to die a lingering death. It seems there is some legal point involved, and if the owner or anyone else should kill him or make use of the meat, or even if they did not make much use of it, the railroad company would not be liable for damages, and the consequence was that the almighty dollar being paramount, the dumb brute had to slowly die, suffering untold tortures from the heat and flies before death came to relieve him. This illustrates that there is something wrong with humanity that one of these days we hope will be rectified. We crossed the Arkansas River along late in the afternoon, having passed numerous Indian villages of squalid and dirty appearance, but still the most civilized of any we had seen, going through the far-famed town of Bushy Head, across the Verdigris River, the waters of which are of a dark green color. We noticed at numerous stations great piles of walnut logs which the Indians had cut and sold to traders holding permits from the Government to trade in the Territory. The train whistled for Red Fork.

Each year after one of our blow-outs, the boys always say, "Now someone ought to write this thing up and have it published, and while it may afford some pleasure to others to read it, it will afford us a great deal in going over and recalling to our minds the events that have taken place in previous years." But it has always been put off, and only odds and ends of the trip have been published from time to time in Forest and Stream. This year I made an agreement with the crowd that if each one would contribute, I would get the thing together and we would see what we could do. Consequently I wrote to the different ones, and I am glad to say they have stuck to their bargain and helped me out.

The following is from the shores of Lake Superior from the Doctor, and we must therefore excuse him.

He writes:

"Marquette, Mich., Dec. 1, 1887. My dear Sir: In answer to your letter of the 28th ult. While thanking you for your kindness, allow me to offer as my excuse the fact that it was my virgin trip and that I am not accustomed to write for the public print, so that I feel that the old campaigners would be better fitted for chronicling the events. (It should be stated that the Doctor did not care much for shooting, and the closing part of his letter is thereby explained, and will throw no discredit on some of the large stories the boys may hereafter tell). As I had no more shooting than one duck while afloat, and a rattlesnake without waiting for him to rise while ashore, I shall have to be classed as a pot hunter, and the severest contest I had was with the Red Fork fleas. With many kind regards to yourself and the boys, I remain,

Yours truly,
THE DOCTOR."

THE JEROME MARBLE PARTY OF WORCESTER, MASS.

Mr. Marble is the third person from the right. From an old photograph sent to me by Mr. Marble many years ago, undated, but it is of the trip of 1883, '84 or not later than '85. They carried a baggage car in addition to this excursion car. I do not know the names of the members of this party other than A. B. Kinney, but they will probably be recognized by old residents of Worcester, Mass.

The next to respond was Genial George. The subjoined recital is his account of what befell us after our arrival at Red Fork.

On Thursday, Oct. 13th, at about 3.00 o'clock in the afternoon, our train drew into the station at Red Fork, in the Indian Territory. The town is situated a short distance below the junction of the Arkansas and Cimarron or Red Fork rivers. The Cimarron is so named from its color which, especially in times of high water, is a deep brick-red. The water of the Cimarron, as is the case with some other streams in the Territory, is brackish and unpalatable.

The town of Red Fork is but a small hamlet, consisting of a few scattering houses, a post office, two or three stores, a blacksmith shop, etc., but no saloon, the sale of liquor or the bringing of it into the Territory being strictly prohibited by Government regulations. The stores carry on the most important and extensive business in this place, as they furnish supplies to the cattle ranches and also to the Indians, some coming a hundred miles or more for their groceries.

A portion of our party made headquarters at the store opposite the station house, and we were surprised at the large, varied and well assorted stock on hand, consisting of almost everything required in housekeeping, except furniture. We found the proprietor of the store a very hospitable and pleasant gentleman who made us feel at home at once. He insisted on our carrying trunks and baggage into the wing of his store, which we converted into a dressing and storage room, and in which we also tied our dogs for the night. After safely disposing of our effects, we began looking about for a place to sleep and for meals. The proprietor tendered the use of a large bed room over the store which would accommodate three of us, and which was accepted with thanks. We then set forth to find a place for the remainder and were directed to the house of a Mrs. M. Upon inquiry we found she had a room and could furnish our meals, so stepping into the back yard and at a bench near the well we made an elaborate toilet by the light of a kerosene lamp and re-entered the house.

Many of us had in our travels met with persons of great and exceptionally marked conversational powers, and some of us even thought we could talk pretty well ourselves, but Mrs. M. soon convinced us that we had all been laboring under a delusion, for from the moment we entered her house until the time of our leaving her talk did not cease for a moment. She gave us her whole history from childhood, that of her husband, a description of the Indians and their habits, and all the gossip of the town for years past. We were all thoroughly subdued, and even the Doctor, who could usually hold his own, was hardly able to edge in a word. We ate our suppers to the running fire of her conversation, and the three who were to sleep at the store hurried away, leaving the Doctor, Jack and myself listening sadly to some unfinished recital. At the store they retired at once, being thoroughly tired out, and slept soundly until awakened long before daylight, at about four o'clock, by the barking of our dogs and the shouts of our trio who had been left at the house. After letting us in, Ed wished to know why they had been routed out at that too early hour. Our answer was that it had been done in self-defense; for after they had left us we retired to the sitting room where our beds were to be made, and Mrs. M. had immediately dropped in on us and continued her conversation for about three hours more, until we were all completely used up. The Doctor at last during a lull was enabled to get in a few words and said, "Now, Mrs. M., if you will kindly retire for a few moments we will go to bed and will then be pleased to have you return and talk us to sleep." To our great joy the hint was taken, and we were not again disturbed until after three o'clock in the morning, when we heard Mrs. M. getting things ready for the early breakfast and busily talking to herself for lack of audience. Being fearful of another attack we arose, and quietly dressing, slipped out of the house and came down to the store. Under the circumstances, Ed readily forgave us for the early call.

While waiting for breakfast we employed our time in getting into our hunting clothes and carrying our trunks and baggage out to the platform in the rear of the store ready to be loaded on the wagon. Breakfast finished and the dogs fed, we bade good-bye to Mrs. M. and returned to the store, where we found awaiting us a double wagon for the baggage and two two-seated "democrat" wagons for ourselves and the dogs. Everything was quickly loaded and at six o'clock we commenced our journey of fifty miles across the reservation of the Creeks to the ranch of the Saginaw Cattle Company situated in the reservation of the Sacs and Foxes. The country through which we passed consisted of beautiful, fertile plains and wooded hills, interspersed with numerous streams and well suited to the raising of stock and ordinary farm crops. Occasionally we passed a house or a cluster of houses and barns where some Indian had settled and fenced in a farm. and in most cases not only were the buildings comfortable, but the crops also seemed to have been properly cared for and were abundant. As we continued, however, the houses became farther and farther apart, and during the last half of the distance not a place of abode was seen from the road, except one or two hunters' tents or camps.

On coming out of one of the plains and ascending a hill we came upon our first game, a covey of quail feeding in the road and in the grass along its side. A halt was called and all was excitement, getting the guns out of their cases and hunting out ammunition belts and boxes from the bottom of the wagons. Giving word to the drivers to hold the dogs, a careful advance was begun, but just before getting within reasonable range, the dogs were by some carelessness let loose and being very rank for want of work, they made a dash into the covey scattering it in every direction. However, each man let go his right and left and a few birds fell. No attempt was made to mark down the others, and only two or three shots were had. Upon gathering up the birds we found that we had secured only seven out of a flock of about twenty, but of course some allowances must be made for the excitement incident to coming upon the game totally unprepared, and also for the action of the dogs. We again started up our teams but took the precaution to have our guns and ammunition ready for action.

No more game was seen, however, for several miles. At last Brown, being on the lookout, called our attention to a large yellowish-red animal about a quarter of a mile ahead of us and to the left of the road, which was evidently intending to cross the road to a deep wooded draw on the right. He would make a few jumps over the tall dead grass and then stand and look toward the wagon. We soon made up our minds that it was a wolf, and Billy taking his long range Bullard rifle got out into a small ravine on our right and ran swiftly forward under cover of its banks to intercept the wolf. We remained quiet in the wagon for some time expecting each minute to hear the crack of the rifle, but all was still. Finally we saw Billy come out on the road ahead of us and about where the wolf crossed. We drove up to him in anything but a good humor, for it seems that he had succeeded twice in getting into position when he had a good sure shot, and each time the rifle snapped so that the wolf escaped unharmed. Upon taking the lock off the rifle, arriving at camp, it was found that for some cause the spring had become weakened and required tempering.

At noon we arrived at Salt Creek, where after driving down one very steep bank, which made the full application of the brakes necessary, and ascending on the other side into a beautiful clump of trees, we unhitched and fed and watered the horses, the stream being salt only in name, and after taking lunch we rested for an hour and again continued our journey through a succession of hills and valleys, and over and across water courses, some dry and others of running water, until just before dark we crossed the stream called the Tiger, which we knew to be only about three miles from the ranch. The country about the Tiger was the wildest we had seen in the Territory, the woods being densely thick, the banks very high and rocky, and as we afterwards found, with plenty of game along its borders. Ascending from the bed of the Tiger to the top of the hill, we followed the road along an elevated plain until we came to a fence which divides the Sacs and Fox and the Creek reservations. Passing through the gate and down the road for a quarter of a mile we arrived at the ranch of the Saginaw Cattle Company where we were welcomed by the inmates, as well as by the baying of two or three "deep-mouthed" hounds. Our baggage wagon did not arrive until the following morning, having broken down while crossing the Tiger.

What we did after our arrival at these "Happy Hunting Grounds" will be given by another member of the party.

GEORGE.

II

THE ranch house of the Saginaw Cattle Company is inside of the fence line about, I should imagine, a mile and a half. It is a one story log house built in three parts, all connected with the regular southern gallery, a midway area roofed with shingles, like the rest of the house. One part is used for a kitchen and dining room, and the other two facing each other, one at the right for the general living room having its big roaring fireplace and best furniture air, the other divided off into sleeping rooms. At the rear is the spring house where the butter, eggs and milk are kept cool, for up out of the solid rock bubbled a clear crystal spring of the usual cold spring temperature. At the rear of the house are the stables in which the team horses and other horses in use are kept. Below is the horse pasture, some 200 or 300 acres fenced in bordering the banks of the Ute. Facing the house is a growth of heavy timber, and at the time we arrived the ground seemed to be literally covered with all kinds of nuts; the squirrels were playing about, the quail calling, and the air was filled with the songs of many birds. On the other side of the ranch from which we approached, gurgled and bubbled a sprightly little creek that wound its crooked path between rocky crevices and joined the river below us. Its steep banks on the other side proved merely a balking spot for the not much to be depended on horses, as we afterward found.

We were warmly welcomed by Jerome and Paine, both members of the Company from our own town, and Coombs, a Tennesseean, who is interested in the ranch. It was the time of the round-up and most of the cowboys were out with the cattle, and the three amateurs had just come in from the last night's camping ground, some fifteen miles beyond, to give us a welcome. The addition of our party made the house rather full, and it was necessary to put up a few beds on the floor. However, as we came on a camping trip this was considered no hardship, but in fact rather something to be appreciated.

The household was looked after by Mrs. Davidson, the wife of the foreman, he being away with the outfit at the round-up. Mrs. Davidson had as an assistant in the kitchen a Creek squaw, with about as villainous a face as one ever saw, and it was a good index to her nature as we afterward learned. She did not seem to take kindly to us, and we heard her tell Mrs. Davidson one day that if we were a sample of the miserable white trash that came down to take the poor Indian's land, she did not wonder that some of them were killed, showing that her disposition was not thoroughly angelic nor cheerful. However, this did not interfere with the Saginaw contingent's consumption of a ton of well cooked rations,

A nice piece of beef had been brought in that day and was well cooked, and with plenty of sweet potatoes and a few vegetables from Mrs. Davidson's kitchen garden, we felt much better and were willing to sit around the open fireplace with our pipes and cigars and discuss the prospects for the coming hunt.

The boys wanted us to join them at the round-up the next day, saying that it would be a sight well worth seeing, and as it was soon to break up, the most favorable opportunity would be on the morrow. This plan was decided upon and soon good nights were said and nothing was to be heard but the melodious snore of the City Official accompanied by a solo on the nasal flute played with good effect by Brooks.

Bright and early we were awake in the morning, the dogs were fed, and all was hurly-burly for the round-up. This is told by the City Official and I will make a little addition thereto after you have read what he has to say on the subject.

"Preparations were made for an early start on the morning after our arrival, and shortly after daylight we set forth, a portion of the party in a two-seated wagon and the remainder, with Messrs. Jerome, Paine and Coombs, mounted on bronchos.

"The distance to where the round up was in progress was about 13 miles, and through as lovely a country as one could wish to see, being very rolling and interspersed with 'draws, which were heavily timbered with oak, pecan, hickory, walnut, etc., but mainly oak, somewhat dwarfed. The weather was simply delightful, a coat of any kind being unnecessary. Between nine and ten o'clock we arrived at the place selected for the round-up, which was a large, level plateau, surrounded by hills with ravines or draws leading up into them. From our station it was a pretty sight, and a very encouraging one to the stock raiser to see in the distance the herders, or cowboys, coming in from every point of the compass driving before them motley colored droves of fine, fat cattle of all ages and sizes.

"In a short time all the herders were in with their charges, and we had before us a crowding, pushing, hooking and bellowing mass of from 3,000 to 4,000 steers; this was the round-up. The next thing in order was the 'cutting out' or selecting from this great herd of all the cattle of proper age and condition for shipment, and this proved to be quite an interesting scene. The herders would ride into the crowd, and selecting a steer which was suitable, would make a dash for it, and notwithstanding the reluctance of the animal to leave its companions, would follow it madly through the herd and finally succeed in driving it out from the others and across the plains for a distance of perhaps 500 yards, where it was taken in charge by two or three cowboys, whose duty was to keep together all the beef cattle 'cut out' from the main herd.

"It seemed quite wonderful to watch the bronchos in this operation. They seemed to follow by instinct the animal selected by the rider and would dodge to and fro in pursuit at full speed through the other thousands of cattle, yet, once put upon the track never made a mistake but kept at the heels of the animal chosen, until it was driven over to the herd of 'cut outs.' The operation of cutting out was continued until all the suitable animals had been selected, when the cowboys, with a whoop and a general charge and cracking of whips drove the remainder of the herd off a quarter of a mile or so, and then left them to scatter over the beautiful pastures until again wanted at the next annual round-up. The beef cattle selected were then driven off to join those which had been cut out at other parts of the range, and the round-up at this point was finished.

"Our party were then invited to ride over to the 'outfit' so called, being a four horse wagon which accompanies the herders and carries the cook, kitchen, blacksmith tools and blankets for the men. We found the outfit about one mile distant under some oaks on the bank of a stream. Dinner was ready, and we all partook heartily and without being particular as to the names of some of the dishes.

"After dinner we witnessed the branding, etc., of some yearlings, which operation appeared to me to be cruel, although undoubtedly necessary. The yearlings were caught by two riders by means of lariats, one being thrown around the neck of the animal and the other around its hindlegs. By means of these ropes it was then thrown, bound and branded.

"The outfit being out of fresh meat, a two-year old steer was shot, butchered and cut up in a rather rough and primitive manner, although the work was rapidly done. The best parts of the meat were placed upon the wagon, and the balance left on the ground for the buzzards and coyotes. The outfit then moved off to be in readiness for another round-up in a different part of the range, on the morrow. Our party remained near the camp for a while after the departure of the wagon, and it was curious to see how soon the buzzards caught sight of the remains of the slaughtered animal, for although when killed, there was scarcely a bird to be seen, yet within fifteen minutes after the wagon drew off, there were scores of them upon and around the carcass, and more coming in every direction as far as the eye could see.

"We then returned to headquarters to be in readiness for our first hunt, which was to begin next day."

The City Official omitted to state that two of the dogs were taken with us that day. After getting some seven or eight miles from the camp, Mose running along by the side of the wagon, suddenly put up his nose and going into a little draw of red top, came to a stiff point and stood there like a picture. Those on horseback turned their heads and finally their horses to see the sight, and we in the wagons hastily tumbled out, put cartridges in our guns and walked four abreast towards where the dog was standing like a rock. We were confident that a whole covey of birds was to be flushed, but such did not prove to be the fact. It was only one old hen and she got up in front of Brooks who very nicely tumbled her over. This was the only one to be found, and after hunting the ground well over, we bundled into the wagon again and went on. Finally topping a high hill, down in the valley before us spread out for a long distance was the cattle herd. In the bright sunlight with the vivid green as a background it was as pretty a picture of moving live colors as one would wish to see. However, this beautiful view and the anticipated pleasure of witnessing a round-up were counter-balanced by something more potent in the minds of Brooks and the writer. I had spent many weary days thumping cattle in Texas and knew too well the process of roping, branding and cutting out. Therefore, when turning to the left in the opposite direction from the herd, we saw meandering through the valley a little water course, fringed on either side with the usual quota of trees and foliage, and noticed that it joined another branch some two miles farther down, and that they both then strove to reach the point where the nooning was to take place at the round-up, the temptation could not be resisted to get out and hunt down its banks, and meet the boys sometime in the middle of the afternoon for the homeward journey. This was all well planned and supposed to have been understood. We understood that we were to go to the top of a high hill midway between the forks of the creek and the round-up, and there await the return of the vehicle did we not get in to their camping place, but this was misunderstood as subsequent events showed.

The day was very warm and after leaving the rest of the party Brooks took the bank and I the bed of the creek, following it along for probably half an hour, when suddenly old Bob came to a point and Mose backed. The trees were very thick at this point and a large covey of quail rose with a whir, disappearing in every direction, and the three shots counted but two birds. They scattered badly and we had very poor luck, getting but four out of the covey.

It became very warm and the dogs could not work if they were away from the water, and this being our first tramp, we were not ambitious, but by and by began to wonder if we had made a mistake in leaving the wagon. One or two coveys of quail were found in this way and our bag began to assume fair proportions. Noon came and passed, and as we came into the valley where we expected to see the round-up ahead of us, not a single animal was in sight. We could not have made a mistake as we had been following the water course, and we had plainly marked it out from the hill top, but where had that immense herd moved and what had become of the party? When anything of this kind takes place one either suddenly becomes very thirsty or very hungry. There was plenty of water near so we could not be thirsty, but we immediately imagined we were starving, and mounting the high hill on which we were, as we supposed, to await the return of the boys, and nothing being in sight we moved farther up to where it was fringed with a thin and scattering growth of scrub oak. The wind by this time had come up, and seemed to be blowing a gale. It was a relief in one sense as it cooled the air, but it made it dangerous to light a fire and we had firmly resolved to have some of our quails broiled before we budged another inch, so we ran the risk. The coals were glowing, and stuck upon a twig, each was holding a bird over the embers. We had no salt, but we did have a little jig water in our flasks and it answered as an excellent substitute. We poured about a tablespoonful over each bird, and I am frank to say that never did a morsel taste better to either of us than these broiled quails with the liquored seasoning. We lit our cigars and stretched out on the grass for half an hour's smoke, and still seeing nothing of the missing party began to be slightly alarmed, when between two hills away off to the left we saw a moving body of cattle. This we were confident was the round-up, and we were sure that the boys must be near there, as the cattle were moving toward the stream and the general direction was where we expected to find them; therefore, we once more hurried to the river bed, and about the same time, finding a nice covey of birds, began to enjoy the sport. Both had made a nice clean right and left and were congratulating each other on our good shooting, when it occurred to us to look at the time and saw that it was nearly three o'clock, an hour past the time for starting home. The situation began to look serious to us, as we were probably fifteen miles from the ranch in a direct line, and what that line was we hardly knew.

Crossing the creek and moving up the hillside toward

where the cattle were going, we saw away in the distance someone riding as if bent on business and coming in our direction. When within hailing distance this proved to be Jerome. He seemed quite excited, saying he had been ransacking the prairie in every direction; that we had not kept to our agreement as to our place of meeting. This was no time for explanations, but he insisted on my taking his horse and riding in the direction he pointed. He said at a certain point I would find Paine waiting, and then I was to take Paine's horse and ride in the direction he was to show me, and he was to bring his horse back to himself and Brooks who would be tramping along in the direction I was to take. Argument was unnecessary and I mounted his horse and set off at a rapid gait. After I had gone about a mile I found Paine, and the rest of the program was carried out. I was directed to a point crossing a ravine and here George was waiting for me and said that the party was a mile or two beyond us and that the City Official and the rest of them had given us up for lost and were very much exercised and afraid that we would have to lie out over night. It was rapidly nearing sundown and there was no track over the prairie to guide us back. Jerome, Paine and Coombs were to stay with the herd for the next day's round-up and then ride into the Agency, some sixty miles distant, and we probably would not see them again while at the ranch, consequently we had no one to pilot us back but our own recollection of the direction taken in the morning.

George and myself rode side by side toward where the wagon was waiting, passing by the way, at the foot of an old dead tree, a dead cow and in a circle around it, in the air and on the trees were probably a thousand turkey buzzards, screaming and fighting for their repast, and making a very weird and uncanny spectacle. The City Official was very much relieved when he saw me with George. Coombs was at the wagon and after Brooks joined us on Jerome's pony, took the two horses back, bidding us good-bye and cautioning us about driving as fast as we could and pointing out the direction to take. We started off feeling quite confident and happy, but had not gone over a mile before one of the horses balked, being played out. Our little jehu, Charlie, had neglected to bring corn enough for his team and they were hungry and fagged out, but he had brought a plentiful supply of tobacco, and if the amount of tobacco juice expectorated could have been equalled by horse food, a good sized livery stable could have been maintained thereon. But it did not seem to worry him, notwithstanding the fact that all of us ripped and profaned considerably. There was nothing to do for it, however, but jump out to see what they would do with the empty wagon. They would pull that, but every time any of us got in they would balk. We were in a hurry and a long ways from home, and it was rapidly growing dark. The City Official being weighty and not given to walking was urged to ride, and finally the jaded nags consented to pull him, and the rest of us swung out at a good pace and really distanced the tired horses. After going four or five miles we struck the main road and then knew the direction home for a certainty. The horses seemed to feel better and the road was easier for them, the evening cooler, and our spirits began to rise, and as if affected in like manner, the horses began to pull us. With much persuasion they were gotten into quite an acceptable trot and we had great hopes of reaching home that night. However, we knew we had to ford the Ute at a very dangerous place, and as it was liable to be a very dark night, this was quite a stumbling block in our way, still, if the horses did not again give out, we were all right. An hour before we had sent the Doctor ahead, he riding a mustang, to try and reach the ranch or Whistler's and send out some fresh horses to us.

We found that by striking up some lively air, and all singing at the top of our voices, the horses were so badly frightened that they dared not stop trotting, or else they appreciated the music so much that they repaid us the best they could. At any rate, when the so-called music commenced, the horses pricked up their ears and quickened their pace. An hour or so rolled by and we were confident we had travelled twenty miles instead of ten, for it certainly was the longest hour's ride I ever had, when out of the black darkness ahead loomed up a light, and it proved to be the Doctor on horseback with a lantern. He said that we were near the ford and we were glad of it. The lantern was carried across ahead of the horses and all jumped out before attempting to ascend the opposite bank, as they would at least pull the empty wagon to the top. We finally arrived home, and were welcomed by the baying of the hounds, and to a more practical extent by Mrs. Davidson's well-cooked supper.

I suppose the incidents that took place that day would have made four times as lengthy an article as this, had I time to narrate them, but this bids fair to be long enough without, and I will describe now the following day's hunt which had been partially agreed upon the night before, but definite arrangements were to be made in the morning.

III

THE place for the day's expedition was decided upon while the horses were being driven in from the pasture and saddled for use. The Doctor and City Official were to ride to the ford of the Ute (pronounced by the natives You-tchay) just below the horse pasture and about half a mile below where the uncertain waters of Prairie Creek join the sluggish flow of the Ute on toward the Cimarron.

Ed and Brooks were to take Mose and strike the Ute a mile or so above the ford at the Whistler ranch, while George and myself were to take Nip and Old Bob and do our duty by the shores of the placid Prairie Creek, striking it as far toward its head as we could while the other party was getting to the agreed starting point. These streams, like most of the creeks or little rivers of this country, are narrow threads of muddy water, in places but two or three yards wide, in others reaches as many rods. The banks are invariably rough, steep and rocky, while the timber consisting of walnut, oak, hickory and pecan, is but a narrow belt of verdure hugging the edges of the sinuous water course. Back of the timber is either the loveliest rolling prairie under the sun, or a little bunch of scrub oak and chaparral, and then the green pasture land. Deer, turkeys and quail are fairly abundant along the water courses, and by striking them about as far up as would make a good day's tramp and carefully hunting toward the fork, and then to the ford where the Doctor and Fred were on guard, we hoped and expected to drive some of the larger game to one another besides filling up the time shooting quail.

At last the poor half-cared for animals, by courtesy called horses, appear. The Doctor and Fred mount and take their departure in one direction and the rest of the party clamber into the hack, as the twelve year old driver, Charley, with a plentiful evacuation of tobacco juice, calls the ordinary two-seated platform spring wagon. The horses, this morning, seem to know they have not far to go and start without the usual balk. Reube is not destined to have his seven days on quail, for Brooks has meat in his eye this morning and not "training vs. breaking." We leave him tied to one of the trunks on the gallery howling and between howls endeavoring to chew up something. This latter feat he successfully accomplishes later in the day to the infinite disgust of Mrs. Davidson, as her dancing pumps will need patching before the season's gaieties are under way. We are off, rattle down the hill, ford the "creek by the house" and painfully the horses tug us up the steep hill on the opposite side. With visions of a former balk in this same spot before us, two of us lighten their load by jumping out. When the top is reached we bowl along at quite a lively gait over the lovely level greensward for a mile or more. We open the gate and pass through the wire of the horse pasture and a little farther George and I leave the hack and strike it afoot across lots for the ground we are to begin on. The boys are lost to sight over the hill beyond. We have not gone far before we hear them banging away, and we know that they have run into quail by the roadside. They tell us that night that after repeated bangings (which we heard and were much blessing our hard luck over) seven birds were brought to bag, a good beginning for the day.

After trudging through the heavily dew-laden grass, for I should judge a mile, we strike the little creek, and after waiting a while for the boys to reach their grounds we start down stream, George taking one bank and I the other. Little Nip hunts close to me this morning and with not too much ambition to tire either of us, but Old Bob is chuck full of his usual store of vim and go and takes in every inch of the ground for 300 yards on either side of the ravine. Ahead four woodducks in radiant plumage spring into the air out of shot and dart down the creek ahead of us. I sing out to George that we will get them next time, and such proves to be the fact, as later on I make two (though I do say it) most extraordinary shots, stopping a duck each time with No. 8's, as I get but a snap shot a good way off with only a shadow of the birds vanishing through the scrub oaks.

It is warm work for us and warmer for the dogs, but as they make a break for the water and take a good swim every little while, they are able to do fair work. We hear an occasional shot from the boys coming down the Ute, and are not idle ourselves as we have made good holes in two coveys that Old Bob has found, and which have been carefully worked out after scattering by Mistress Nip.

The noonday sun is hot overhead and we must be nearing the forks where Ed and Brooks promised to wait for us should they get there first, when suddenly Miss Nippy is all awake. For some time she had not taken much interest in the proceedings, but now what ails the dog? With nose up she is quartering the ground at a rapid gait from the water's edge to the prairie edge of the post oaks. For here the ground is quite rough and covered with small acorns, just the spot for turkeys. Suddenly she stops undecided which way to turn, and before I have time to call out for George, up gets a big turkey from a bunch of green tangle on the hillside fifty yards ahead. I suddenly realize that I have only three-quarters of an ounce of No. 8 in my little 16 bore and curse my luck. The turkey flies straight for the cover along the creek ahead, and as he crosses in front of me, I pull on him well to the front and have the satisfaction of seeing him drop all of a heap. I shout my good luck to George across the ravine and tell Nip to fetch, but as the turkey is thrashing around at a great rate, she can't get hold of him until Old Bob takes a hand, and proudly half drags and half carries the bird to me. Miss Nippy thinks she has done it and says so as plainly as a dog can, which is plain enough for me. She shakes herself, jumps up on me, and gives vent to several loud yawns or youws. I now imagine that the other boys must have gotten a flock of turkeys scattered at the forks and this one was skulking over here, so I am on the lookout for more. After cautioning George I send Old Bob down into the creek bed, and at once up jumps a big fellow before he had time to stop, out of my reach, but goes directly over George and not twenty feet high, but Mr. George has disregarded my caution, and is sitting down with his gun between his legs, lighting his pipe. He tumbles over, bangs his gun and never touches him, though he swears feathers flew at the second shot. We all of us do this on principle, and no one can contradict the assertion. After talking the matter over, we concluded that this bird had gone across the river and there was no use following him at present.

Expecting to meet the boys and not knowing whether they had gone to the ranch or were still above us, we sat down on the banks where the two streams joined and awaited developments, first to wait for the boys to join us and next we wished to see if any turkeys would call. After sitting in this way about twenty minutes and not hearing anything, I took up a turkey call and gave a few yelps. Nothing was heard but the silence of the prairie back of us and the woodlands ahead. Again it was repeated with like results, and about discouraged, after waiting for a few moments I tried it again, when away off on the other banks of the stream I heard a yelp in response. Soon I had them calling all around me and they seemed to be coming in my direction, when with a bow-wow-wow the dogs gave notice of the approach of someone through the sumac, and sure enough there was Shorty sent from the house on horseback to hunt us up. The others had come in and had had their dinner and were waiting for us at the ranch to finish the day's hunt in another direction. Of course the dogs' barking had interfered with the turkey calling. We got Shorty off from his horse, and all quieted down, and waiting a little while soon had the turkeys calling again, but the opposition from an old gobbler on the other side that could call louder than myself, made the flock instead of joining me join him, and majestically move over the hill in the distance.

We crossed over, and Shorty on his pony circled around in ahead of them and succeeded in getting them scattered. When they are frightened this way and skulking they lie to a dog like a quail, and it is fine sport to hunt them over points. But about four out of six I always miss because I get so excited that the birds seem bigger than all outdoors, and where my shot goes I do not know. This proved to be the case today and three or four good shots were missed. However, among us we secured three turkeys and sent Fred back for the boys to come up on the other side of the stream and hunt along its bank, as we were certain turkeys would be found there. They joined us an hour afterward, but with poor success.

George and I were walking along the bank of the river discouraged and giving up all hope of finding any more, when suddenly I looked down below us and saw Old Bob as stiff as a rock pointing toward an old clump of leaves just beyond me. Calling out to George to watch out, that there was a turkey there to a dead certainty, I started toward him when up rose a gobbler of huge proportions and started directly over the river. Our guns both cracked at the same time and he tumbled over, striking in mid stream. Bob was told to fetch him and he swam out to him and took hold with a vim, but with the turkey's floundering and flopping and the weight of the bird and the running water, the chances were very much in favor of the dog's being drowned unless he let go of the bird. Under and over they went. Every time he would attempt to raise him, the turkey would flop in his death struggles and sink the dog out of sight. Miss Nippy stood on the bank whining, and recognizing her companion's trouble plunged in and swam to him and took hold of the bird's wing, and side by side they swam to the shore.

This ended the day's sport as far as we were concerned and we were very well satisfied, having had a long tramp and a very comfortable bag. The others, however, got into a very large covey of quail and we heard them banging away like a Fourth of July fusilade, and of course thought they would come in with a bag full, but it seems their markmanship was poor, and when counting the birds at night we found that George and I had discounted the others.

A funny thing happened to the party on the other side of the river this afternoon. As they were riding along with guns loaded with fine shot, not ten feet ahead of Brooks' horse, up jumped a fine deer, and without standing on ceremony bounded over the prairie and disappeared. No one thought of shooting, but all of them wished they had had buckshot or a rifle or something of the sort. After much talk and hilarity on the subject they moved ahead, but had not gone more than thirty feet when the performance was repeated, a deer jumping out from under the nose of the Doctor's horse, and going away with the same freedom as the other. This happened to us several times while we were at the ranch, but we were never prepared for them and did not have any luck. The only way to do is to make a business of hunting deer and nothing else, then you will have your rifle ready and not be bothered with fine shot when once within shooting distance.

Each day's hunt was only a repetition of the one just described. The City Official rather beat us on elegant and artistic shots, but in the bottom lands it was so hot the dogs could not work well and the quail were sure to pitch into some miserable tangle where it was impossible to get more than one or two shots at them, and we finally concluded after shooting three or four days, that we had had enough of the quail.

We had expressed a desire to more closely examine a turkey buzzard. We knew it was against the law to kill one, but we were anxious to know more about them and finally concluded that we would kill just one in the interest of science, though we did not break the law as the sequel will show. Going home one afternoon from a long jaunt down the Cimarron, we noticed above us a long and continuous flight of these black noiseless birds, sailing one after another in the same direction. George cracked away at one of them and I did also, but somehow or other it seemed to have no effect on them for they really must have been a long ways off, but in this clear atmosphere a bird of ordinary size will look very near when really it is out of gunshot. The City Official picked up my 16 bore with the remark that he would show them how it was done and pulled on one that was sailing overhead. It doubled up like a jackknife and fell near us. Of course we supposed it was a dead bird and gingerly pulled out three or four of the large symmetrical quills from the wing and examined the bird and were about to throw it to one side as a dirty piece of rubbish, when without a word of warning it suddenly gave a flop and sailed off, seemingly as well as ever. It was like the Irishman's toad, "Be jabbers, but you would be a fine bird had I not shot your feathers off." We had a hearty laugh over this incident and congratulated ourselves that we had gained the information desired and not broken any law.

We reached the ranch that night in good spirits, having had an excellent day's jaunt, and we were ready for the homeward journey on the morrow. The boys concluded that it was best to divide up the party, and after packing our baggage, each being supplied from the generosity of Shorty with a box holding half a peck or so of the nicest pecans anyone ever tasted, we prepared to say good-bye to this pleasant spot.

WM. B. MERSHON

IV

THE way of getting back to Red Fork will be described by both Brooks and Ed. You will readily see that the stories do not jibe; one or the other is given to romancing, and we are afraid it is "Section 37;" at any rate he must stand the brunt of it. Ed's is given first as he, together with George and the writer, left ahead of the others, consequently he must know more about what took place. In fact, Brook's little episode of the "night sentinel" business at our camping ground that night will probably be better relished by first hearing a truthful account of the same. Ed writes as follows:

"On Monday we decided to make a start for home the next day, and arranged that Billy, George and Ed should start at noon with the lumber wagon and darky driver, taking the baggage and dogs. George, thinking he would rather ride in the saddle than the wagon, we concluded to take a saddle horse along. As we would have a pretty heavy load, we figured on making Buck Horn Creek, about fifteen miles from the ranch, the first day which would leave us an easy drive of about thirty miles for Wednesday. The rest of the party were to leave on Wednesday morning with the spring wagon and make the drive through in a day.

"Tuesday morning was occupied in packing our trunks and getting ready for an early start, intending

THE HANGING OF THE DEER

From painting by Courtier owned by Edwin C. Nichols of Battle Creek.

Left to right: Hiram T. Merrill, Johnstown, Barry County, Michigan; John Nichols of Battle Creek.

to get our dinner about eleven and pull right out so as to get into camp before dark, but we found it after twelve before we were ready for the start.

"After bidding a regretful goodbye to the good people at the ranch, we climbed to our seats and George mounted his horse, saying he would ride ahead and have the gate open for us. We directed our driver to go ahead, but we did not seem to go with any great rush, our off horse evidently not having been getting ready as the rest of us had, or for some reason he did not like to leave home. It was only after much coaxing and many endearing words added to many kind remarks from the rest of our party and the friends at the ranch such as, "Boys, we hate to see you go off in such a hurry;" "Say, boys, does your father want to sell that horse?" "Wood and water right handy; this will be a good place for you to camp tonight," and other equally cheering remarks that we finally got under way. But just as we came to the farther end of the corral and not yet out of sight of the ranch, the same horse stopped again, probably to take a last sad look at the home of friends he loved so well. About this time George, having tired of holding the gate open for us, rode back to see if we had decided to wait over until next day. We told him to go back and hold the gate, we were coming as fast as we could, wondered if he took us for an express train. We stuffed our fists in our ears so as not to hear the flattering and encouraging remarks from our friends at the ranch, and calmly awaited the result of our driver's conference with the refractory beast. After a while it resulted satisfactorily, for we again got under way and this time managed to get outside the gate and out of sight of the ranch. That was about as far as we did get though, as again not half a mile from the ranch our poor homesick horse finally made up his mind that he could not leave his home and pull his share of the load, and he stopped evidently never to go again. Any inducements we had to offer only seemed to settle him more firmly in his determination to that effect. We finally asked our driver if among all the horses in the pasture there was not one that would pull.

"Golly, boss, doan know; dare dat hoss, M. C., mebby he pull; he mighty peart hoss." So Ed rode back to the ranch, and getting Fred and Shorty, rode over to the pasture and after some little time succeeded in capturing "dat are hoss, M. C." and taking him back to the wagon hitched him in. Thinking perhaps two balky horses might be better than one in case M. C. should turn out that way, we took the saddle off the horse George had been riding and put it on the homesick one, sending the other back to the pasture. This time we made a glorious start; at least it seemed so to us who had been so long trying to come so far. After this we had no more trouble with our horses, getting along over the smooth roads at a good fair rate of speed.

"We had gone about five or six miles on our way, when Billy sang out, "See the turkeys," and off to our right about two hundred yards was a flock of about thirty-five or forty, making tracks as fast as they could for the thick timber in the creek bottom, about four hundred yards ahead. We called out to George, who was a short distance ahead, to ride into the flock and scatter them. He put spurs to his horse and dashed ahead, riding right into the midst of them before they took wing. He unfortunateliy did not have his gun with him. A portion of the birds flew out of sight into the thick timber, but many of them after flying a short distance, lit and skulked in the thick grass. Billy and Ed immediately unchained the three dogs, Bob, Nip and Mose, and loading with our No. 2 shells, started after them. Billy had marked them down better than Ed and seemed to be right on the track of them for they began getting up ahead of him but flushing wild and giving him long shots, evidently too long and out of reach, although he kept his little sixteen going, hoping he might be able to reach one of them. This he finally did, breaking its wing and crippling it so that the dogs captured it. This seemed to make our dogs perfectly crazy with excitement, so bad in fact that for sometime we could do nothing with them. They flushed a number of birds and about spoiled our sport. Finally, however, we succeeded in calling them in and after giving them a sound chastising and some good advice, we succeeded in quieting them down to a great extent.

"By this time we had come down into the creek bottom, and while skirmishing around Mose came to another point, backed beautifully by Bob and Nip. Billy and Ed walked up, and when they were within about fifteen yards of the dogs, up got a fine large turkey right from under Mose's nose, when bang, bang, bang, bang, four shots were fired in rapid succession and still the turkey kept on his way apparently none the worse for the leaden shower the boys supposed they had sent in his direction and which was intended for his especial benefit. To say that those two men were disgusted with themselves and with each other would not begin to express their frame of mind. To think that two men of their age who had shot in the field every season since they were big enough to raise a gun to their shoulder, and considered themselves at least fair shots, would allow a bird of that size and as fair a shot as could be to get up and go away without so much as a feather to show, was decidedly humiliating. The dogs each turned around and looked upon them with amazement, and as much as said, "Well, a bit of that chastisement you administered to poor us would evidently have done you good. "Billy and Ed, after gazing sorrowfully for a few moments upon each other and then upon the vacant spot where the bird had disappeared over the brow of the hill, called for George and asked him the nearest way to the wagon, and took a bee line therefor. On the way Mose again came to a point, and upon walking up, there rose a solitary quail which Ed proceeded to pulverize with a charge of No. 2 shot. Had it been a turkey, he probably would have missed it. Had we taken the time and not have been in so much of a hurry and only taken one dog, we could have bagged a good portion of the flock, but thinking we would just rush in and get a shot or two apiece and then hurry on our road—as it was getting late in the afternoon—we did not take the pains we otherwise would.

"Hurrying to the wagon we told the driver to make as good time as possible so as to get over some bad road which we had to cross before getting to our camping place. Darkness overtook us some miles before reaching the Buck Horn, and by the time we stopped at the stream it was pitch dark. We crossed the stream by the light of matches, and reaching the other bank proceeded to look for a place to camp, or rather to prowl around in the dark, and by the aid of a match now and then to find a place where fuel was handy. We soon found it, and quickly had a roaring fire of dry oak limbs, which we found in great abundance scattered around on the ground. It was certainly as good a place for a camp as we could have found had we had broad daylight to aid us. While our driver was watering and feeding his horses the rest of us were gathering wood, of which we got a generous supply, after which we proceeded to discuss the lunch which had been put up for us by Mrs. Davidson—a cold lunch, but a supper which we all appreciated and relished. After supper Billy and Ed, taking a firebrand for a torch, took some dog biscuit down to the creek to soak for the dog's breakfast, placing them in a shallow place in the stream and weighting them down with heavy stones to prevent their floating away. We made our camp by placing the trunks and boxes at our heads to break the wind, and placing our rubber blankets on the ground, using our overcoats for pillows, each one of us rolling up in a pair of blankets, we slept the sleep of tired, happy men with the bright stars shining down upon us and the festive voice of the coyote and screech owl soothing our slumbers.

"We had intended starting in the morning before break of day but it was fairly light before we were astir, and after sunrise before we were under way. On going to the creek to perform our morning toilets, we took the dogs along to give them their biscuits for breakfast, but alas, some hungry animal had made a raid upon the biscuits during the night and not a solitary one remained. We had to share our own breakfast with the dogs.

"While getting ready to start we heard a covey of quail calling. They were on our way. We took the dogs and started ahead of the team. Our dogs worked beautifully, making several fine points. We had a number of shots, bagging several of them.

"We saw no more game until about the middle of the forenoon when we flushed a fine large turkey from the side of the road, not twenty feet from the wagon. Of course, we were not ready to shoot; our guns were at hand but not loaded. It flew about two hundred yards and lit, taking to her heels for the prairie. George came to the wagon and got his gun and attempted to ride her down, but before he came within shot she took wing and flew over the hills out of sight. This was the last game we saw on the way out.

"Just before reaching Salt Creek, where we intended taking our noon-day lunch, the other boys with the light wagon overtook us, so we had a jolly dinner all together.

"After dinner and a rest of about an hour and a half we started out together, but the spring wagon soon left us out of sight and we saw no more of them until we reached Red Fork.

"We stopped during the afternoon and gathered a lot of hickory nuts, filling our pockets with the largest, finest nuts we had ever seen, being at least twice the size of our Michigan nuts. Walnuts, hickory nuts and pecans grow in great abundance. The pecans, like the hickory nuts, grow very large and are of very rich, sweet flavor.

"We reached Red Fork soon after dark, tired but having enjoyed our ride every minute and regretting that we were so soon to leave this beautiful country. I think we would all have been glad to turn right around and take the trip over again, had not business cares required our attention elsewhere."

ED.

Now hold your breath, for truly friend Brooks proceeds to mix things up.

"After we decided to turn our faces homeward the next question was how we were to divide up, as we had considerable baggage, consisting of our trunks, valises, ammunition, blankets, etc., and only one little, two-seated platform and a common lumber wagon; the former the natives called a stage, and in one sense it was, taking into consideration the size of the horses used in that country.

"The drive being an all day one, we started the lumber wagon on with the baggage and dogs, the team being an old rheumatic horse and a mule, with Tom, the colored boy, as driver escorted by George mounted on a mustang and Ed and Billy as passengers. They got off at noon, and the rest of the party promised to follow early in the morning and overtake them and all go in to Red Fork together.

"Tom, with the aid of a little nip and now and then from his passengers' "cold tea" urns, succeeded in making good headway and reached a splendid camping ground on the bank of a very pretty stream before dusk. (Reader, pause and prepare to admire a very fertile imagination). Cutting down a large tree for the back log of the camp fire, they took the trunks, boxes and valises from the wagon and placed them so as to form a half circle facing the fire. Each gathered a quantity of dry leaves and made his bed, first placing the leaves on the ground, then a blanket over the rubber cloth and blankets over themselves, using grain bags stuffed with leaves for pillows. Each man in turn stood guard two hours during the night, which passed very pleasantly, being first serenaded by a pack of wolves and followed by a company of coyotes and a pair of horned owls.

"At daylight Tom, who was on guard roused the

sleepers with, "Gemman, for de lord sake, jes hear dem dar turkeys." And sure enough, not more than fifty yards away they found a flock of some forty, and in less than an hour they succeeded in making a fine bag. Returning to camp they found Tom busy getting out the cooking utensils preparatory to getting breakfast, after which they broke camp and started on their journey.

"About this time the Doctor, Fred or the Official as we called him, Morley and the boy driver, Charley, left the ranch with the two-seated platform and the little jaded mustangs. After they had driven about ten miles the off horse showed signs of a general giving out, so Morley took the reins, thinking perhaps with good, careful driving they might be able to reach Red Fork. The roads for the next twelve miles were very rough stony ground with a good many hills to climb. At the foot of each hill the party would get out, Morley with the whip in one hand and the reins in the other, while Fred, the Doctor and Charley put their shoulders to the rear of the wagon and pushed. With this assistance, all the mustangs had to do was to "keep in the middle of the road" until the top of the hill was reached. We traveled along in this manner until we passed all the rough places and were once more upon the rolling prairie with the advance party just in sight. At noon we overtook them on the bank of a little creek.

"Tom, having had to stand watch the night before and do the driving too, the strain had been a little too much for him; there he lay stretched out full length, flat on his back and fast asleep. The mule, horse and George's mustang were enjoying a good feed of corn, while Ed, Billy and George were busy getting the coffee boiling and preparing one of the turkeys for the fry pan. When Charley's team had been unhitched, the harness taken off and each mustang had had his "roll," they were given their corn, and all hands joined in getting ready for one of Mershon's square meals.

"Should you, dear reader, ever have the pleasure of camping out with brother Mershon, you would be greatly interested in watching him prepare his meals. Delmonico's French cook would open his eyes could he see the unrivalled way in which our brother dresses and cooks his birds and fish.

"After dinner cigars were brought out and some good stories were told, with now and then an old chestnut, a little snooze all around, and then the party was off.

"After going some few miles the dogs to our left came to a point. Morley having his gun ready, jumped out and ran over to where they were and got two barrels into a covey of chickens. Motioning us to follow, he struck out for the birds, which had gone some distance. In crossing a little slough where the grass was above his waist he was seen to suddenly stop, and clapping his hands to his leg he yelled like a loon, "Come, boys, come quick. Centipede, centipede. Come quick." Charley and Tom put their whips to their beasts and away we flew, George taking the lead on his mustang, and expecting every minute to see

Morley fall. But judge of our surprise when on getting out and coming up to him we found his fingers closely clutched on his deerfoot hunting knife, which had worked its way through his trousers pocket. He was as pale as a ghost and frightened almost to death. Some of the boys were so convulsed with laughter that it was necessary to administer restoratives in order to prevent hysterics. Poor Morley will never forget that day as long as he lives, and we will never forget that heartrending yell he gave.

"Returning to the road we resumed our journey. The sun was coming down pretty hot about this time, and we began to feel the need of water for ourselves and teams. Morley all this time had been very quiet; the centipede scare seemed to have completely sealed him up. He ventured a remark now and then but tended strictly to his driving.

"After making up our minds we would have to go without water until we reached Red Fork, there suddenly loomed up in the distance a little white farmhouse. It seemed ages before we reached it, the distance being much greater than it looked, and owing to the poor condition of our teams each mile was seemingly the last they would be able to make. We found the place deserted, doors locked and curtains down, and made up our minds the owners, Indian farmers, were in town trading. We found the well. The water was very good indeed for that country. Taking a drink all round and giving the mustangs all they could hold, we began to explore the premises. The Official mounted an old hen coop and with his field glasses sighted a watermelon patch in the corner of an old garden a few rods from the road leading from the house to the main. Getting into our wagons we proceeded in the direction of the patch. In the meantime some of the boys were debating the advisability of tackling said patch, fearing one of the red men might have been left to watch the farm and at this moment be in some convenient place to give us the full benefit of a Winchester. The City Official, going a good deal on his glass and having made a careful survey, expressed himself fully satisfied that no red man was within gunshot. On the strength of this, three of the party volunteered to go into the patch and bring out two melons each, Fred agreeing to keep a sharp lookout and give the alarm by firing his six-shooter. They did not take a great deal of pains in selecting their plunder as they appeared anxious to return as soon as possible. Putting the melons in the bottom of the hack and covering them with a blanket we proceeded.

"Upon losing sight of the farmhouse and seeing no one approaching from either direction, we halted and prepared for a feast. The Doctor suggested we should be very careful not to let any of the seeds drop in the road as we might be tracked. One after another of the melons were cut, but out of the six we failed to find a ripe one. Having the six green melons on our hands we commenced to question how to dispose of them. It would not do to carry them into Red Fork, and to leave them by the roadside would never do, so after looking the matter all over we decided to get out our axes, dig a hole for each one and bury them. This we did, leaving six little newly made graves behind us.

"Nothing worthy of note transpired during the rest of our journey that day, and a little after dark we drew up to Hotel de Miller, tired, yet sorry it was our last day with the birds."

BROOKS.

He sends with his romance the following, and I think you will agree with me in saying this being his "first offense" will not excuse his utter disregard of truth:

"Dear Editor (meaning me)—Inclosed please find my first effort. Should you find after reading it through too "rank" for publication, consign it to the base burner and forever spare me ever making another attempt at this kind of business. Yours truly,

BROOKS.

The shadows of an October evening had gathered around the good village of Red Fork as we pulled up our tired horses at the store door. For the last hour we had expected the lights of the little station to appear at each bend in the road, and finally as we swung into the quiet little valley, shut off on all sides by the curving hills now dark against the sky, and saw glimmering in the distance the dozen lights that told us that there was Red Fork, we gave a great sigh of relief all around, for really the wagon seats had grown very, very hard.

A lantern is kindly provided by our good storekeeper, and by its light we unload the wagon, tie up the dogs, proceed to quiet Mrs. Miller's for supper, and oh, how hungry we are. The same kerosene lamp and bucket of water with slimy laundry soap accompaniment is again resorted to and we take turns at it, cheered by the tuneful voice of our fair hostess which oozes through the cracks and crevices of the kitchen where she is busy frying sweet potatoes—and such potatoes. We forgave her then, and forgive her again now for all the tiresome hours we were compelled to listen, or rather, hear her chattering tongue—and the fried sweet potatoes did it. You who have never eaten a potato grown in the Creek Nation, and especially one of Mrs. M's frying, are not qualified to mention the vegetable. How we did cause everything put before us to disappear. The fragrant tobacco makes the world look very peaceful to us all. We feed the hungry dogs and they go to sleep at once. A turkey is taken to Mrs. M. with the request that it be cooked for our tomorrow's lunch, for we have had one experience with Vanita at the dinner hour. We pack everything we can, and turn in and sleep the sleep of all good sportsmen under similar circumstances.

After breakfast next morning we finish the packing. Brooks shaves himself and has no competitor in the dude line. I learn this by his completely cutting me out with a fair damsel in a trim fitting corduroy suit who fortunately had an entire seat to herself as we changed that night at Monett. Brooks of course could find no other in the coach after I, the only really eligible man in the crowd, had been rudely sat down upon by her.

Brooks leaves us at Springfield to spend a few days in his old home at Fort Scott, taking the sorrowful dog Rube. We awaken next morning at St. Louis. The boys want to spend a day here, and I am in a hurry to be back to a business needing my attention. We say good-bye and I proceed on my way with the three dogs and reach home in good time the following morning.

So ends the event of the year, that which we had counted upon for weeks and weeks before going, and will with pleasant memories look back upon for months, and who knows but for years afterward.

These yearly pilgrimages of the same chosen friends and boon companions can not go on forever. One by one time obliterates a dear face or hushes the sunny, cheering voice of the best of friends. A thousand and one things are possible, and some more than probable to prevent, that will make even the next round-up, on which we are already counting, not what the last was. Some may be gone, and a pleasure will be blemished with regret. Which one this will be may many years to come be called upon to tell, and though taking our life's pleasure year by year as we grow older, can we not hope that many a time again may the old clan gather at the call of the spirit of the golden October days, and not a single leaf be torn from the book of our fellowship.

WM. B. MERSHON.

Dec. 1887

www.ingramcontent.com/pod-product-compliance
Lightning Source LLC
LaVergne TN
LVHW011201110826
845150LV00006B/1280